ASSESSING RESEARCH–DOCTORATE PROGRAMS

A METHODOLOGY STUDY

WITHDRAWN
UTSA LIBRARIES

Jeremiah P. Ostriker and Charlotte V. Kuh, Editors

Assisted by James A. Voytuk

Committee to Examine the Methodology
for the Assessment of Research-Doctorate Programs

Policy and Global Affairs Division

NATIONAL RESEARCH COUNCIL
OF THE NATIONAL ACADEMIES

THE NATIONAL ACADEMIES PRESS
WASHINGTON, D.C.
www.nap.edu

THE NATIONAL ACADEMIES PRESS   500 Fifth Street, N.W.   Washington, DC 20001

NOTICE: The project that is the subject of this report was approved by the Governing Board of the National Research Council, whose members are drawn from the councils of the National Academy of Sciences, the National Academy of Engineering, and the Institute of Medicine. The members of the committee responsible for the report were chosen for their special competences and with regard for appropriate balance.

This study was supported by the National Institutes of Health Award# N01-OD-4-2139, Task Order No. 107, received support from the evaluation set-aside Section 513, Public Health Act; the National Science Foundation Award# DGE-0125255; the Alfred P. Sloan Foundation Grant No. 2001-6-10, and the United States Department of Agriculture Award# 43-3AEM-1-80054 (USDA-4454). Any opinions, findings, conclusions, or recommendations expressed in this publication are those of the author(s) and do not necessarily reflect the views of the organizations or agencies that provided support for the project.

International Standard Book Number 0-309-09058-X (Book)
International Standard Book Number 0-309-52708-2 (PDF)
Library of Congress Control Number 2003113741

Additional copies of this report are available from the National Academies Press, 500 Fifth Street, N.W., Lockbox 285, Washington, DC 20055; (800) 624-6242 or (202) 334-3313 (in the Washington metropolitan area); Internet, http://www.nap.edu

THE NATIONAL ACADEMIES
Advisers to the Nation on Science, Engineering, and Medicine

The **National Academy of Sciences** is a private, nonprofit, self-perpetuating society of distinguished scholars engaged in scientific and engineering research, dedicated to the furtherance of science and technology and to their use for the general welfare. Upon the authority of the charter granted to it by the Congress in 1863, the Academy has a mandate that requires it to advise the federal government on scientific and technical matters. Dr. Bruce M. Alberts is president of the National Academy of Sciences.

The **National Academy of Engineering** was established in 1964, under the charter of the National Academy of Sciences, as a parallel organization of outstanding engineers. It is autonomous in its administration and in the selection of its members, sharing with the National Academy of Sciences the responsibility for advising the federal government. The National Academy of Engineering also sponsors engineering programs aimed at meeting national needs, encourages education and research, and recognizes the superior achievements of engineers. Dr. Wm. A. Wulf is president of the National Academy of Engineering.

The **Institute of Medicine** was established in 1970 by the National Academy of Sciences to secure the services of eminent members of appropriate professions in the examination of policy matters pertaining to the health of the public. The Institute acts under the responsibility given to the National Academy of Sciences by its congressional charter to be an adviser to the federal government and, upon its own initiative, to identify issues of medical care, research, and education. Dr. Harvey V. Fineberg is president of the Institute of Medicine.

The **National Research Council** was organized by the National Academy of Sciences in 1916 to associate the broad community of science and technology with the Academy's purposes of furthering knowledge and advising the federal government. Functioning in accordance with general policies determined by the Academy, the Council has become the principal operating agency of both the National Academy of Sciences and the National Academy of Engineering in providing services to the government, the public, and the scientific and engineering communities. The Council is administered jointly by both Academies and the Institute of Medicine. Dr. Bruce M. Alberts and Dr. Wm. A. Wulf are chair and vice chair, respectively, of the National Research Council.

www.national-academies.org

COMMITTEE TO EXAMINE THE METHODOLOGY FOR THE ASSESSMENT OF RESEARCH-DOCTORATE PROGRAMS

JEREMIAH P. OSTRIKER, *Committee Chair,* Princeton University; Cambridge University, UK
ELTON D. ABERLE, University of Wisconsin-Madison
JOHN I. BRAUMAN, Stanford University
GEORGE BUGLIARELLO, Polytechnic University
WALTER COHEN, Cornell University
JONATHAN COLE, Columbia University
RONALD GRAHAM, University of California-San Diego
PAUL W. HOLLAND, Educational Testing Service
EARL LEWIS, University of Michigan
JOAN F. LORDEN, University of North Carolina-Charlotte
LOUIS MAHEU, University of Montréal
LAWRENCE B. MARTIN, Stony Brook University
MARESI NERAD, University of Washington
FRANK SOLOMON, Massachusetts Institute of Technology
CATHARINE R. STIMPSON, New York University

Board on Higher Education and Workforce Liaison

JOHN D. WILEY, University of Wisconsin-Madison

NRC Staff

CHARLOTTE KUH, Deputy Executive Director, Policy and Global Affairs Division, and Study Director
PETER HENDERSON, Director, Board on Higher Education and Workforce
JAMES VOYTUK, Senior Project Officer
HERMAN ALVARADO, Research Associate
TERESA BLAIR, Senior Project Assistant
EDVIN HERNANDEZ, Program Associate
ELAINE LAWSON, Program Officer
ELIZABETH SCOTT, Office Assistant
EVELYN SIMEON, Administrative Associate

PANEL ON TAXONOMY AND INTERDISCIPLINARITY

WALTER COHEN, *Panel Co-Chair,* Cornell University
FRANK SOLOMON, *Panel Co-Chair*, Massachusetts Institute of Technology
ELTON D. ABERLE, University of Wisconsin-Madison
RICHARD ATTIYEH, University of California-San Diego
GEORGE BUGLIARELLO, Polytechnic University
LEONARD K. PETERS, Virginia Polytechnic Institute and State University
ROBERT F. JONES, Association of American Medical Colleges

PANEL ON QUANTITATIVE MEASURES

CATHARINE R. STIMPSON, *Panel Chair,* New York University
RONALD GRAHAM, University of California-San Diego
MARSHA KELMAN, University of Texas, Austin
LAWRENCE B. MARTIN, Stony Brook University
JEREMIAH P. OSTRIKER, Princeton University; Cambridge University, UK
CHARLES E. PHELPS, University of Rochester
PETER D. SYVERSON, Council of Graduate Schools

PANEL ON REPUTATIONAL MEASURES AND DATA PRESENTATION

JONATHAN COLE, *Panel Co-Chair,* Columbia University
PAUL HOLLAND, *Panel Co-Chair,* Educational Testing Service
JOHN BRAUMAN, Stanford University
LOUIS MAHEU, University of Montréal
LAWRENCE MARTIN, Stony Brook University
DONALD B. RUBIN, Harvard University
DAVID SCHMIDLY, Texas Tech University

PANEL ON STUDENT PROCESSES AND OUTCOMES

JOAN F. LORDEN, *Panel Chair,* University of North Carolina-Charlotte
ADAM FAGEN, Harvard University
GEORGE KUH, Indiana University, Bloomington
EARL LEWIS, University of Michigan
MARESI NERAD, University of Washington
BRENDA RUSSELL, University of Illinois-Chicago
SUSANNA RYAN, Indiana University, Bloomington

Acknowledgments

This study has benefited enormously from the advice of countless students, faculty, administrators, and researchers in government and industry who have sent us e-mail, especially concerning the taxonomy and our questionnaires. The Council of Graduate Schools, the National Association of State Universities and Land Grant Colleges, the National Academy of Sciences, the GREAT Group of the American Association of Medical Colleges, and the Association of American Universities all invited us to their meetings when the study was in its early stages and helped us to formulate the major issues the Committee needed to address. Nancy Diamond, Ron Ehrenberg, and the late Hugh Graham also were helpful to us in the early stages.

We owe an immense debt to our pilot site universities and their graduate deans, institutional researchers, and faculty who helped us differentiate between the desirable and the feasible. These are: Florida State University, Michigan State University, Rensselaer Polytechnic Institute, The University of California-San Francisco, The University of Maryland, The University of Southern California, The University of Wisconsin-Milwaukee, and Yale University.

We are grateful to the National Research Council Staff: Herman Alvarado, Teresa Blair, Edvin Hernandez, Evelyn Simeon, and Elizabeth Scott. They made our meetings run smoothly, helped produce the report, and amassed the data without which the Committee would not have been able to do its work. Irene Renda at Princeton University and Jeanette Gilbert at the University of Cambridge also assisted these efforts by ably supporting the Committee's Chair.

This report has been reviewed in draft form by individuals chosen for their diverse perspectives and technical expertise, in accordance with procedures approved by the NRC's Report Review Committee. The purpose of this independent review is to provide candid and critical comments that will assist the institution in making its published report as sound as possible and to ensure that the report meets institutional standards for objectivity, evidence, and responsiveness to the study charge. The review comments and draft manuscript remain confidential to protect the integrity of the deliberative process.

We wish to thank the following individuals for their review of this report: Leslie Berlowitz, American Academy of Arts and Sciences; Terrance Cooper, University of Tennessee; Nancy Diamond, Pennsylvania State University; Edward Hiler, Texas A&M University; Louis Lanzerotti, Bell Laboratories, Lucent Technologies; Edward Lazowska, University of Washington; Brendan Maher, Harvard University; Risa Palm, University of North Carolina-Chapel Hill; C. Kumar Patel, Pranalytica, Inc.; Gerald Sonnenfeld, Morehouse School of Medicine; Stephen Stigler, University of Chicago; Kathleen Taylor (Retired), General Motors Corporation; E. Garrison Walters, Ohio Board of Regents; Pauline Yu, American Council of Learned Societies; and James Zuiches, Washington State University.

Although the reviewers listed above have provided many constructive comments and suggestions, they were not asked to endorse the conclusions or recommendations, nor did they see the final draft of the report before its release. The review of this report was overseen by Ronald Ehrenberg, Cornell University, and Lyle Jones, University of North Carolina-Chapel Hill. Appointed by the National Research Council, they were responsible for making certain that an independent examination of this report was carried out in accordance with institutional procedures and that all review comments were carefully considered. Responsibility for the final content of this report rests entirely with the authoring committee and the institution.

Finally, we wish to thank our funders: the National Institutes of Health, the National Science Foundation, the Alfred P. Sloan Foundation, and the United States Department of Agriculture. Without their support, both financial and conceptual, this report would not have been written.

Contents

List of Tables and Charts

TABLES

CHARTS

Executive Summary

EXECUTIVE SUMMARY

The Committee to Examine the Methodology to Assess Research-Doctorate Programs was presented with the task of looking at the methodology used in the 1995 National Research Council (NRC) Study, *Research-Doctorate Programs in the United States: Continuity and Change* (referred to hereafter as the "1995 Study"). The Committee was asked to identify and comment on both its strengths and its weaknesses. Where weaknesses were found, it was asked to suggest methods to remedy them.

The strengths of the 1995 Study identified by the Committee were:

- *Wide acceptance.* It was widely accepted, quoted, and utilized as an authoritative source of information on the quality of doctoral programs.
- *Comprehensiveness.* It covered 41 of the largest fields of doctoral study
- *Transparency.* Its methodology was clearly stated.
- *Temporal continuity.* For most programs, it maintained continuity with the NRC study carried out 10 years earlier.

The weaknesses were:

- *Data presentation.* The emphasis on exact numerical rankings encouraged study users to draw a spurious inference of precision.
- *Flawed measurement of educational quality.* The reputational measure of program effectiveness in graduate education, derived from a question asked of faculty raters, confounded research reputation and educational quality.
- *Emphasis on the reputational measure of scholarly quality.* This emphasis gave users the impression that a "soft" criterion, subject to "halo" and "size effects," was being overemphasized for the assessment of programs.

- *Obsolescence of data.* The period of 10 years between studies was viewed as too long.
- *Poor dissemination of results.* The presentation of the study data was in a form that was difficult for potential students to access and to use. Data were presented but were neither interpreted nor analyzed.
- *Use of an outdated or inappropriate taxonomy of fields.* Particularly for the biological sciences, the taxonomy did not reflect the organization of graduate programs in many institutions.
- *Inadequate validation of data.* Data were not sent back to providers for a check of accuracy.

The Committee recommends that the NRC conduct a new assessment of research-doctorate programs. This study will be conducted by a committee appointed once funding for the new assessment has been assured. The membership for this future committee may well overlap to some degree the membership of the current committee, but that is a matter to be decided by the NRC President. The recommendations that appear below should be carefully considered by that committee along with other viable alternatives before final decisions are made. In particular, in the report that follows, some recommendations are explicitly left to the successor committee. The taxonomy and the list of subfields, as well as details of data presentation, should be carefully reviewed before the full study is undertaken.

The 1995 Study amassed a vast amount of data, both reputational and quantitative, about doctoral programs in the United States. Its data were published as a 700-page book with downloadable Excel table files from the NRC website. Later, in 1997, it became available on CD-ROM. Because the study was underfunded, however, very little analysis of the data could be conducted by the NRC committee. Thus, the current Committee was asked not only to consider the rationale for the study, the kind of data that should be collected, and how the data should be presented but also to recommend what data analyses should be conducted in order to make the report more useful and to consider new, electronic means of report dissemination.

Before the study was begun, the presidents of organizations forming the Conference Board of Associated Research Councils and the presidents of three organizations representing graduate schools and research universities[1] met and discussed whether another assessment of research doctoral programs should be conducted at all. They agreed to the following statement of purpose:

> The purpose of an assessment is to provide common data, collected under common definitions, which permit comparisons among doctoral programs. Such comparisons assist funders and university administrators in program evaluation and are useful to students in graduate program selection. They also provide evidence to external constituencies that graduate programs value excellence and assist in efforts to assess it.

In order to fulfill that purpose, the NRC obtained funding and formed a committee,[2] whose statement of task was as follows:

> The methodology used to assess the quality and effectiveness of research doctoral programs will be examined and new approaches and new sources of information identified. The findings from this methodology study will be published in a report, which will include a recommendation concerning whether to conduct such an assessment using a revised methodology.

The Committee conducted the study as a whole, informed through the deliberations of panels in each of four areas:

• Taxonomy and Interdisciplinarity

The task of this panel was to examine the taxonomies used to identify and classify academic programs in past studies, to identify fields that should be incorporated into the next study, and to determine ways to describe programs across the spectrum of academic institutions. It was asked to develop field definitions and procedures to assist institutions in fitting their programs into the taxonomy. In addition, it was to devise approaches intended to characterize interdisciplinary programs.

• Quantitative Measures

This panel was charged with the identification of measures of scholarly productivity, educational environment, student and faculty characteristics, and with finding effective methods for collecting data for these measures. In particular, it was asked to identify measures of scholarly productivity, funding, and research infrastructure, which could be field-specific if necessary, as well as demographic information about faculty and students, and characteristics of the educational environment—such as graduate student support, completion rates, time to degree, and attrition. It was asked specifically to examine measures of scholarly productivity in the arts and humanities.

• Student Processes and Outcomes

The panel was asked to investigate possible measures of student outcomes and the environment of graduate education. It was to determine what data could be collected about students and program graduates that would be comparable across programs, at what point or points in their education students should be surveyed, and whether existing surveys could be adapted to the purpose of the study.

• Reputational Assessment and Data Presentation

The task of this panel was to critique the method of measuring reputation used in the 1995 Study, to consider whether reputational measures should be presented at all, and to examine alternative ways of measuring and presenting scholarly reputation. It was to consider the possible incorporation of industrial, governmental, and international respondents into the reputational assessment process. Finally, it was to decide on new methods for presenting reputational survey results so as to indicate appropriately the statistical uncertainty of the ratings.

The panels made recommendations to the full committee, which then accepted or modified them as recommendations for this report.

The Panel on Quantitative Measures and the Panel on Student Processes and Outcomes developed questionnaires for institutions, programs, faculty, and students. Eight diverse institutions volunteered to serve as pilot sites.[3] Their graduate deans or provosts, with the help of their faculties, critiqued the questionnaires and, in most cases, assisted the NRC in their administration. Their feedback was important in helping the Committee ascertain the feasibility of its data requests.

---

[1]These were: John D'Arms, president, American Council of Learned Societies; Stanley Ikenberry, president, American Council on Education; Craig Calhoun, president, Social Science Research Council; and William Wulf, vice-president, National Research Council. They were joined by: Jules LaPidus, president, Council of Graduate Schools; Nils Hasselmo, president, Association of American Universities; and Peter McGrath, president, National Association of State Universities and Land Grant Colleges.

[2]The study was funded by the National Institutes of Health, the National Science Foundation, the United States Department of Agriculture, and the Alfred P. Sloan Foundation.

[3]These were: Florida State University, Michigan State University, Rensselaer Polytechnic Institute, University of California-San Francisco, University of Maryland, University of Southern California, University of Wisconsin-Milwaukee, and Yale University. The type of participation varied from institution to institution, from questionnaire review to administration as well as review of questionnaires.

Because of the transparent way in which NRC studies present their data, the extensive coverage of fields other than those of professional schools, their focus on peer ratings, and the relatively high response rates they obtain, the Committee concluded that there is clearly value added in once again undertaking the NRC assessment. The question remains whether reputational ratings do more harm than good to the enterprise that they seek to assess.

Ratings would be harmful if, in giving a seriously or even somewhat distorted view of the graduate enterprise, they were to encourage behavior inimical to improving its quality. The Committee believes that a number of steps recommended in this report will minimize these risks. Presenting ratings as ranges will diminish the focus of some administrators on hiring decisions designed purely to "move up in the rankings." Ascertaining whether programs track student outcomes will encourage programs to pay more attention to improving those outcomes. Asking students about the education they have received will encourage a greater focus by programs on education in addition to research. Expanding the set of quantitative measures will permit deeper investigations into the components of a program that contribute to a reputation for quality. A careful analysis of the correlates of reputation will improve public understanding of the factors that contribute to a highly regarded graduate program.

Given its investigations, the Committee arrived at the following recommendations:

Recommendation 1: The assessment of both the scholarly quality of doctoral programs and the educational practices of these programs is important to higher education, its funders, its students, and to society. The National Research Council should continue to conduct such assessments on a regular basis.

Recommendation 2: Although scholarly reputation and the composition of program faculty change slowly and can be assessed over a decade, quantitative indicators that are related to quality may change more rapidly and should be updated on a regular and more frequent basis than scholarly reputation. The Committee recommends investigation of the construction of a synthetic measure of reputation for each field, based on statistically derived combinations of quantitative measures. This synthetic measure could be recalculated periodically and, if possible, annually.

Recommendation 3: The presentation of reputational ratings should be modified so as to minimize the drawing of a spurious inference of precision in program ranking.

Recommendation 4: Data for quantitative measures should be collected regularly and made accessible in a Web-readable format. These measures should be reported whenever significantly updated data are available. (See Recommendation 4.1 for details.)

Recommendation 5: Comparable information on educational processes should be collected directly from advanced-to-candidacy students in selected programs and reported. Whether or not individual programs monitor outcomes for their graduates should be reported.

Recommendation 6: The taxonomy of fields should be changed from that used in the 1995 Study to incorporate additional fields with large Ph.D. production. The agricultural sciences should be added to the taxonomy and efforts should be made to include basic biomedical fields in medical schools. A new category, "emerging fields," should be included.

Recommendation 7: All data that are collected should be validated by the providers.

Recommendation 8: If the recommendation of the Canadian Research-Doctorate Quality Assessment Study, which is currently underway, is to participate in the proposed NRC study, Canadian doctoral programs should be included in the next NRC assessment.

Recommendation 9: Extensive use of electronic Web-based means of dissemination should be utilized for both the initial report and periodic updates (cf. Recommendations 2 and 4).

DETAILED RECOMMENDATIONS

Taxonomy and Interdisciplinarity

The recommendations concern the issue of which fields and which programs within fields should be included in the study. Generally, the Committee thought that the numeric guidelines used in the 1995 Study were adequate. Although the distribution of Ph.D. degrees across fields has changed somewhat in the past 10 years, total Ph.D. production has remained relatively constant. Thus, it was concluded that there is no argument for changing the numeric guidelines for inclusion unless a field that had been included in past studies has significantly declined in size.

Recommendation 3.1: The quantitative criterion for inclusion of a field used in the preceding study should be, for the most part, retained—i.e., 500 degrees granted in the last 5 years.

Recommendation 3.2: Only those programs that have produced five or more Ph.D.s in the last 5 years should be evaluated.

Recommendation 3.3: Some fields should be included that do not meet the quantitative criteria, if they had been included in earlier studies.

Doctoral programs in agriculture are in many ways similar to programs in the basic biological sciences that have always been included. Recognizing this fact, schools of agriculture convinced the Committee that their research-doctorate programs should be included in the study along with the traditionally covered programs in schools of arts and sciences and schools of engineering. In addition, programs in the basic biomedical sciences may be in either arts and science schools or in medical schools. A special effort should be made to assure that these programs are covered regardless of administrative location.

Recommendation 3.4: The proposed study should add research-doctorate programs in agriculture to the fields in engineering and the arts and sciences that have been assessed in the past. In addition, it should make a special effort to include programs in the basic biomedical sciences that are housed in medical schools.

A list of the fields recommended for inclusion is given in Table ES-1, at the end of the Executive Summary.

Recommendation 3.5: The number of fields should be increased, from 41 to 57.

The Committee considered the naming of broad categories of fields and made recommendations on changes in nomenclature for the next report.

Recommendation 3.6: Fields should be organized into four major groupings rather than the five in the previous NRC study. Mathematics/Physical Sciences are merged into one major group along with Engineering.

Recommendation 3.7: Biological Sciences, one of the four major groupings, should be renamed "Life Sciences."

The actual names of programs vary across universities. The Committee agreed that, especially for diverse fields, the names of subfields should be provided to assist institutions in assigning their diversely named fields to categories in the NRC taxonomy and to aid in an eventual analysis of factors that contribute to reputational ratings.

Recommendation 3.8: Subfields should be listed for many of the fields.

Although there is general agreement that interdisciplinary research is widespread, doctoral programs often retain their traditional names. In addition, interdisciplinary programs will vary from university to university in whether their status is stand-alone or whether they are a specialization in a broader traditional program. The Committee believes that it would assist potential students in identifying these programs, regardless of location, if it introduced a new category: *emerging field(s)*. The existence of these fields should be noted and, whenever possible, data about them should be collected and reported, but their heterogeneity, relatively brief historical records, and small size would rule out conducting reputational ratings since they are not established programs.

Recommendation 3.9: Emerging fields should be identified, based on their increased scholarly and training activity (e.g., race, ethnicity, and post-Colonial studies; feminist, gender, and sexuality studies; nanoscience; computational biology). The number of programs and degrees, however, is insufficient to warrant full-scale evaluation at this time. Where possible, they should be included as subfields. In other cases, they should be listed separately.

The Committee wished to recognize a particular class of interdisciplinary program, "global area studies." These are programs that study a particular region of the world and include faculty and scholars from a variety of disciplines.

Recommendation 3.10: A new broad field, "Global Area Studies," should be included in the taxonomy and include as subfields: Near Eastern, East Asian, South Asian, Latin American, African, and Slavic Studies.

Quantitative Measures

Data collection technology and information systems have vastly improved since the 1995 Study. Although the Committee wishes to minimize respondent burden, it concluded that collecting additional quantitative measures would assist users in characterizing programs and in understanding the correlates of reputation.

Recommendation 4.1. The Committee recommends that, in addition to data collected for the 1995 Study, new data be collected from institutions, programs, and faculty. These data are listed in Table 4-1 in Chapter 4.

Student Processes and Outcomes

The Committee concluded that all programs should periodically survey their students about their experiences and perceptions of their doctoral programs at different stages during and after completing their doctoral studies, and that programs in different universities should be able to compare the results of such surveys. It also recognized that to conduct these surveys and to achieve response rates that would permit program comparability for 57 fields would be prohibitively expensive. Thus, it recommended that a questionnaire for graduates be designed and made available for program use (Appendix D) but that the proposed NRC study should only administer a questionnaire, targeting students admitted to candidacy in selected fields.

Recommendation 5.1: The proposed NRC study of research-doctorate programs should conduct a survey of enrolled students in selected fields who have advanced to candidacy for the doctoral degree regarding their assessment of their educational experience, their research productivity, program practices, and institutional and program environment.

Although potential doctoral students are intensely interested in the career outcomes of recent graduates of programs that they are considering and although professional schools routinely track and report such outcomes, such reporting is not usual for research-doctorate programs. The Committee concluded that such information, if available, would provide a useful way of distinguishing among programs and be helpful to comparative studies that wish to group programs that prepare students for similar kinds of employment. The Committee also concluded that *whether* a program collects and makes available employment outcomes data useful to potential students would be an indicator of responsible educational practice.

Recommendation 5.2: Universities should track the career outcomes of Ph.D. recipients both directly upon program completion and at least 5-7 years following degree completion in preparation for a future NRC doctoral assessment. A measure of whether a program carries out and publishes outcomes information for the benefit of prospective students and as a means of monitoring program effectiveness should be included in the next NRC assessment of research-doctorate programs.

Reputational Measures and Data Presentation

The part of the NRC assessment of research-doctorate programs that receives a lion's share of attention, both from the general public and within academia, is the presentation of survey results of scholarly quality of programs. Often these results are viewed as simply a "horse race" to determine which programs come in first or are in the "top 10." In truth, many factors contribute to program reputation, and earlier studies have failed to identify what they might be. What the Committee views as the overemphasis on ranking has encouraged the pursuit of strategies that will "raise a program in the rankings" rather than encourage an investigation of the determinants of high-quality scholarship and how that should be preserved or improved. Toward this end, the Committee recommends that the next report emphasize rating rather than ranking and include explicit measurement

of the variability across raters as well as analyses of the factors that contribute to scholarly quality of doctoral programs. Furthermore, in reporting ranking, appropriate attention should be paid to statistical uncertainties. This recommendation, however, rejects the suggestion that reputational ratings should be totally discarded.

Recommendation 6.1: The next NRC survey should include measures of scholarly reputation of programs based on the ratings by peer researchers in relevant fields of study.

The Committee applied and developed two statistical techniques that yield similar results to ascertain the variability in ratings of scholarly quality.

Recommendation 6.2: Resampling methods should be applied to ratings to give ranges of rankings for each program that reflect the variability of ratings by peer raters. The panel investigated two related methods, one based on Bootstrap resampling and another closely related method based on Random Halves, and found that either method would be appropriate.

The Committee concluded that the study could be made more useful to both general users and scholars of higher education if it provided examples of analytical ways in which the study data could be used.

Recommendation 6.3: The next study should have sufficient resources to collect and analyze auxiliary information from peer raters and the programs being rated to give meaning and context to the rating ranges that are obtained for the programs. Obtaining the resources to collect such data and to carry out such analyses should be a high priority.

After examining how closely the measure of effectiveness in doctoral education ("E") correlates with the measure of scholarly quality of program faculty ("Q") in the 1995 Study, the Committee agreed that "E" should be dropped from the next study. Another qualitative measure, the change in program quality in the last 5 years ("C") should be replaced by the change in "Q" between studies for those programs and fields that were included in both studies.

Recommendation 6.4: The proposed survey should not use the two reputational questions on educational effectiveness (E) and change in program quality over the past 5 years (C). Information about changes in program quality can be found from comparisons with the previous survey analyzed in the manner we propose for the next survey.

Although in some fields the traditional role of doctoral programs as trainers of the professoriate continues, in many other fields a growing proportion of doctorates takes up positions in government, industry and in academic institutions that are not research universities. The Committee was undecided whether and how information from these sectors might be obtained and incorporated into the next study and leaves it as an issue for the successor committee.

Recommendation 6.5: Expanding the pool of peer raters to include scholars and researchers employed outside of research universities should be investigated with the understanding that it may be useful and feasible only for particular fields.

There are very few doctoral programs that will admit that their mission is anything other than to train "world-class scholars." Yet it is clear that different programs prepare their graduates to teach and conduct research in a variety of settings. Programs know who their peer programs are. Thus, rather than ask programs to declare their mission, the Committee concluded that it would be most useful to provide the programs themselves with the capability to select their own peers and carry out their own comparisons.

Recommendation 6.6: The ratings should not be conditioned on the mission of the programs, but data to conduct such analyses should be made available to those interested in using them.

The Committee wondered whether raters would rate programs differently if they had more information about the program faculty members and their productivity. The Committee recommends an investigation of this question.

Recommendation 6.7: Serious consideration should be given to the cues that are given to peer raters. The possibility of embedding experiments using different sets of cues given to random subsets of peer raters should be seriously considered in order to increase the understanding of the effects of cues.

Different raters have different degrees of information about the programs that they are asked to rate, even if all they are given is a list of faculty names. The Committee would like to see an investigation of the nature and effects of familiarity on reputational ratings.

Recommendation 6.8: Raters should be asked how familiar they are with the programs they rate and this information should be used both to measure the visibility of the programs and, possibly, to weight differentially the ratings of raters who are more familiar with the program.

TABLE ES-1 Recommended Fields for Inclusion

Life Sciences
    Biochemistry, Biophysics, and Structural Biology
    Molecular Biology
    Developmental Biology
    Cell Biology
    Ecology and Evolutionary Biology
    Microbiology
    Genetics, Genomics, and Bioinformatics
    Immunology and Infectious Disease
    Neuroscience and Neurobiology
    Pharmacology, Toxicology, and Environmental Health
    Physiology
    Plant Sciences
    Food Science and Food Engineering
    Nutrition
    Entomology
    Animal Sciences
Emerging Fields
    Biotechnology
    Systems Biology

Physical Sciences, Mathematics, and Engineering
    Aerospace Engineering
    Biological and Agricultural Engineering
    Biomedical Engineering
    Chemical Engineering
    Civil and Environmental Engineering
    Electrical and Computer Engineering
    Operations Research, Systems Engineering, and Industrial Engineering
    Materials Science and Engineering
    Mechanical Engineering
    Astrophysics and Astronomy
    Chemistry
    Computer and Information Science
    Earth Sciences
    Mathematics
    Applied Mathematics
    Oceanography, Atmospheric Sciences, and Meteorology
    Physics
    Statistics and Probability
Emerging Fields
    Nanoscience and Nanotechnology
    Information Science

Arts and Humanities
    American Studies
    History of Art, Architecture, and Archaeology
    Classics
    Comparative Literature
    English Language and Literature
    French Language and Literature
    German Language and Literature
    History
    (Linguistics moved to Social and Behavioral Sciences)
    Music
    Philosophy
    Religion
    Spanish and Portuguese Language and Literature
    Theatre and Performance Studies
    Global Area Studies
Emerging Fields:
    Race, Ethnicity, and Post-Colonial Studies
    Feminist, Gender, and Sexuality Studies
    Film Studies

Social and Behavioral Sciences
    Anthropology
    Communication
    Economics
    Agricultural and Resource Economics
    Geography
    (History moved to Arts and Humanities)
    Linguistics
    Political Science
    Psychology
    Sociology
Emerging Field
    Science and Technology Studies

1

Introduction

Assessments of the quality of research-doctorate programs and their faculty are rooted in the desire of programs to improve quality through comparisons with other similar programs. Such comparisons assist them to achieve more effectively their ultimate objective—to serve society through the education of students and the production of research. Accompanying this desire to improve is a complementary goal to enhance the effectiveness of doctoral education and, more recently, to provide objective information that would assist potential students and their advisors in comparing programs. The first two goals emerged as graduate education began to grow before World War II and as higher education in the United States was transformed from a predominantly elite enterprise to the widespread and diverse enterprise that it is today. The final goal became especially prominent during the past two decades as doctoral training expanded beyond training for the professoriate.

As we begin a study of methodology for the next assessment of research-doctorate programs, we have stepped back to ask some fundamental questions: Why are we doing these rankings? Whom do they serve? How can we improve them? This introduction will also serve to provide a brief history of the assessment of doctoral programs and report on more recent movements to improve doctoral education.

A SHORT HISTORY OF THE ASSESSMENT OF RESEARCH-DOCTORATE PROGRAMS

The assessment of doctorate programs in the United States has a history of at least 75 years. Its origins may date to 1925, a year in which 1,206 Ph.D. degrees were granted by 61 doctoral institutions in the United States. About two-thirds of these degrees were in the sciences, including the social sciences, and most of the remaining third were in the humanities. Yet, Raymond M. Hughes, president of Miami University of Ohio and president of the Association of American Colleges, said in his 1925 annual report:

At the present time every college president in the country is spending a large portion of his time in seeking men to fill vacancies on the staff of his institution, and every man [president] is confronted with the question of where he can hope to get the best prepared man of the particular type he desires.[1]

Hughes conducted a study of 20 to 60 faculty members in each field and asked them to rank about 38 institutions according to "esteem at the present time for graduate work in your subject."

Graduate education continued to expand, and from time to time, reputational studies of graduate programs were carried out. These studies limited themselves to "the best" programs and, increasingly, those programs that were excluded complained about sampling bias.

In the 1960s, Allan Cartter, vice president of the American Council on Education, pioneered the modern approach for assessing reputation, which was used in the 1982 and 1993 NRC assessments. He sought to include all major universities and, instead of asking raters about the "esteem" in which graduate programs were held, he asked for qualitative judgments of three kinds: 1) the quality of the graduate faculty, 2) the effectiveness of the doctoral program, and 3) the expected change in relative position of a program in the next 5 to 10 years.[2] In 1966, when Cartter's first study appeared, slightly over 19,000 Ph.D.s were being produced annually in over 150 institutions.

Ten years later, following a replication of the Cartter study by Roose and Anderson in 1970, another look at the methodology to assess doctoral programs was undertaken under the auspices of the Conference Board of Associated Research Councils.[3] A conference on assessing doctoral

---

[1]Goldberger, et al., eds. (1995:10).
[2]Cartter (1966).
[3]Consisting of the Social Science Research Council, the American Council of Learned Societies, the American Council on Education, and the National Research Council.

programs concluded that raters should be given the names of faculty in departments they rate and that "objective measures" of the characteristics of programs should be collected in addition to the reputational measures. These recommendations were followed in the 1982 assessment that was conducted by the National Research Council (NRC).[4] By this time, over 31,000 doctorates were being produced by over 300 institutions, of which 228 participated in the NRC study.

The most recent NRC assessment of doctorates, conducted in 1993 and published in 1995, was even more comprehensive. The 1995 Study design tried to maintain continuity with the 1982 measures, but it added and refined quantitative measures. With the help of citation and publication data gathered by the Institute for Scientific Information (ISI), it expanded the measures of publications and citations. It also included measures of awards and honors for the humanities. It covered 41 fields in 274 institutions, and data were presented for 3,634 doctoral programs.

This expansion, however, did not produce a noncontroversial set of rankings. It is widely asserted that "halo" effects give high rankings to programs on the basis of recognizable names—star faculty—without considering average program quality. Similarly, there is evidence to support the contention that programs within well-known, larger universities may have been rated higher than equivalent programs in lesser-known, smaller institutions. It is further argued that the reputational rankings favor already prestigious departments, which may be, to put it gently, "past their prime," while de-emphasizing striving programs that are investing in achieving excellence. Another criticism involves the inability of the study to recognize the excellence of "niche" and smaller programs. It is also asserted that, although reputational measures seek to address scholarly achievement as something separate from educational effectiveness, they do not succeed. The high correlation between these two measures supports this assertion.

Finally, and most telling, there is criticism of the entire ranking business. Much of this criticism, directed against rankings published by a national news magazine, attacked those annual rankings as derived from capricious criteria constructed from varying weights of changing variables. Fundamentally, the incentives created by any system of rankings were said to induce an emphasis on research productivity and scholarly ranking of faculty to the detriment of another important objective of doctoral education—the training of the next generation of scholars and researchers. Rankings were said to create a "horse race" mentality in which every doctoral program, regardless of its mission, was encouraged to emulate programs in the nation's leading research universities with their emphasis on research and the production of faculty who focused primarily on research. At the same time, a growing share of Ph.D.s were setting off for

careers outside research universities and, even when they did take on academic positions, taught in institutions that were not research universities. As Ph.D. destinations changed, the question arose whether the research universities were providing appropriate training.

Calls for Reforms in Graduate Education

Although rankings may be under fire from some quarters, this report comes at a time when such an effort can be highly useful for U.S. doctoral education generally. Recently, there have been numerous calls for reform in graduate education. Although based on solid research about selected programs and their graduates, these calls lack a general knowledge base that can inform recommendations about, for example, attrition from doctoral study, time to degree, and completion. Further, individual programs find it difficult to compare themselves with similar programs. Some description of the suggested graduate education reforms can help to explain why a database, constructed on uniform definitions and collected in the same year, could be helpful both as a baseline from which reform can be measured and as a support for data-based discussions of whether reforms are needed.

In the late 1940s, the federal government was concerned with the need for educating a large number of college-bound World War II veterans and created the National Science Foundation to support basic science research at universities and to fund those students interested in pursuing advanced training and education. Competition with the Russians, the battle to win the Cold War, and the sense that greater expertise in science and engineering was key to America's interests jumpstarted a new wave of investments in the 1960s, resulting in a tripling of Ph.D.s in science and engineering during that decade. Therefore, for nearly a quarter of a century those calling for change asked universities to expand offerings and capacity in areas of national need, especially in scientific fields.[5]

By the mid-1970s, a tale of two realities had emerged. The demand for students pursuing doctoral degrees in the sciences and engineering continued unabated. At the same time, the number of students earning doctoral degrees in the humanities and social sciences started a decade-long drop, often encouraged by professional associations worried by gloomy job prospects and life decisions based on reactions to the Vietnam War (for a period graduate school insured military service deferment). Thus, a presumed crisis for doctorates in the humanities and humanistic social sciences was appearing as early as the 1970s. Nonetheless, the overall number of doctoral recipients quadrupled between 1960 and 1990.[6]

By the 1990s a kind of conversion of perspectives emerged. Rapid change in technologies, broad geopolitical

---
[4]Jones et al. (1982).

[5]Duderstadt (2000); Golde (July 2001 draft).
[6]Duderstadt (2000: 91); Bowen and Rudenstine (1992:8-12, 20-55).

factors, and intense competition for the best minds led scientific organizations and bodies to call for the dramatic overhaul of doctoral education in science and engineering. For the first time, we questioned whether we had overproduced Ph.D.s in certain scientific fields. Meanwhile, worry about lengthening times to degree, incomplete information on completion rates, and less-than-desirable job outcomes led to plans to reform practices in the humanities, the arts, and the social sciences.

A number of these reform efforts have implications for the present NRC study and should be briefly highlighted. The most significant statement in the area of science and engineering policy came from the Committee on Science, Engineering and Public Policy (COSEPUP), formed by the National Academy of Sciences, the National Academy of Engineering, and the Institute of Medicine. Cognizant of the career options that students follow (more than half in non-university settings), the COSEPUP report, *Reshaping the Graduate Education of Scientists and Engineers (1995)*, called for graduate programs to offer more versatile training, recognizing that only a fraction of the doctoral recipients become faculty members. The committee encouraged more training programs to emphasize more and better mentoring relationships. The report called for programs to continue emphasizing quality in the educational experience, monitor time to degree, attract a more diverse domestic pool of students, and make expectations as transparent as possible.

The COSEPUP report took on the additional task of segmenting the graduate pathways. It acknowledged that some students would stop after a master's degree, others would complete a doctorate, and others would complete a doctorate and have significant research careers. The committee suggested different graduate expectations and outcomes for students, depending upon the pathway chosen. To assist this endeavor the committee called for the systematic collection of pertinent data and the establishment of a national policy conversation that included representatives from relevant sectors of society—industry, the Academy, government, and research units, among others. The committee signaled the need to pay attention to the plight of postdoctoral fellows, employment opportunities in a variety of fields, and the importance of attracting talented international students.[7]

Three years later the Pew Charitable Trust funded the first of three examinations of graduate education. Re-envisioning the Ph.D., a project headed by Professor Jody Nyquist and housed at the University of Washington, began by canvassing stakeholders—students, faculty, employers, funders, and higher education associations. More than 300 were interviewed, five focus groups were created, e-mail surveys went to six samples, and a mail survey was distributed. Nyquist and her team brought together representatives of this group for a two-day conference in 2000. Since that meeting the project has continued as an active website for the sharing of best practices.

The project began with the question, "How can we re-envision the Ph.D. to meet the societal needs of the 21st century?" It found that representatives from different sectors had different emphases. On the whole, however, there was the sense that, while the American-style Ph.D. has great value, attention is needed in several areas. First, time to degree must be shortened. For scientists this means incorporating years as a postdoctoral fellow into an assessment of time to degree.[8] Second, the pool of students seeking doctorates needs to be more diverse, especially through the inclusion of more students of color. Third, doctoral students need greater exposure to information technology during their careers. Fourth, students must have a more varied and flexible curriculum. Fifth, interdisciplinary research should be emphasized. And sixth, the graduate curriculum should include a broader sense of the global economy and the environment. The project and call for reforms built on Woodrow Wilson National Fellowship Foundation President Robert Weisbuch's assessment that "when it comes to doctoral education, nobody is in charge, and that may be the secret of its success. But laissez-faire is less than fair to students and to the social realms that graduate education can benefit." The project concluded with the recommendation that a more self-directed process take place. Or in the words of Weisbuch, "Re-envisioning isn't about tearing down the successfully loose structure but about making it stronger, more particularly asking it to see and understand itself."[9]

The Pew Charitable Trusts also sponsored research that assessed students as well as their concerns and views of doctoral education as another way of spotlighting the need to reform doctoral education. Chris Golde and Timothy Dore surveyed doctoral students in 11 fields at 27 universities, with a response rate of 42.5 percent, yielding nearly 4,200 respondents. The Golde and Dore study (2001), *At Cross Purposes*, concluded that "the training doctoral students receive is not what they want, nor does it prepare them for the jobs they take." They also found that "many students do not clearly understand what doctoral study entails, how the process works and how to navigate it effectively."[10]

A Web-based survey conducted by the National Association of Graduate and Professional Students (NAGPS) produced similar findings. Students expressed tremendous satisfaction with individual mentoring but some pointed to a mismatch between their graduate school education and the jobs they took after completing their dissertation. Responses,

---

[7]Committee On Science, Engineering, and Public Policy (1995).

[8]A study by Joseph Cerny and Maresi Nerad replaced time to degree with time to first tenure and found remarkable overlap between science and non-science graduates of UC Berkeley 10 years after completion of the doctorate.

[9]Nyquist and Woodford (2000:3).

[10]Golde and Dore (2001:9).

of course, varied from field to field. Most notably, students called for more transparency about the process of earning a doctorate, more focus on individual student assessments, and greater help for students who sought nontraditional jobs.[11] Both the Golde and Dore study and the NAGPS survey asked various constituent groups to reassess their approaches in training doctoral students.

Pew concluded its interest in the reform of the research doctorate with support to the Woodrow Wilson National Fellowship Foundation. The Foundation was asked to provide a summary of reforms recommended to date and offer an assessment of what does and could work. The Woodrow Wilson Foundation extended this initial mandate in two significant ways.

First, it worked with 14 universities in launching the Responsive Ph.D. project.[12] All 14 institutions agreed to explore best practices in graduate education. To frame the project, participating schools agreed to look at partnerships between graduate schools and others sectors, to diversify the pool of students enrolled in doctoral education, to examine the paradigms for doctoral training, and to revise practices wherever appropriate. Specifically, the project highlighted professional development and pedagogical training as new key practices. The architects of the effort believed that improved professional development would better match student interests and their opportunities. They sensed an inattentiveness to pedagogical training in many programs and believed more attention here would benefit all students. Concerned with the insularity or narrowing decried by many interviewed by the Re-envisioning the Ph.D. project, the Responsive Ph.D. project invited participants concerned with new paradigms to address matters of interdisciplinarity and public engagement. They were encouraged to hire new people to help remedy the relative underrepresentation of students of color in most fields besides education. The project wanted to underscore the problem and encourage imaginative, replicable experiments to improve the recruitment, retention, and graduation of domestic minorities. Graduate programs were encouraged to work more closely with representatives of the K-12 sectors, community colleges, four-year institutions other than research universities, foundations, governmental agencies, and others who hire doctoral students.[13]

Second, the Responsive Ph.D. project advertised the success of various projects through publications and a call for a fuller assessment of what works and what does not. Former Council of Graduate Schools (CGS) President Jules LaPidus observed, "Universities exist in a fine balance between being responsive to 'the needs of the time' and being responsible for preserving some vision of learning that transcends time."[14] To find that proper balance the project proposed national studies and projects.

By contrast, the Carnegie Initiative, building on the same body of evidence that fueled the directions championed by the Responsive Ph.D. project, centered the possibilities for reform in departments. After a couple of years of review, the initiative settled on a multiyear project at a select number of universities in a select number of disciplines. Project heads, Lee Shulman, George Walker, and Chris Golde, argue that cultural change, so critical to reform, occurs in most research universities in departments. Through a competitive process, departments in chemistry, mathematics, English, and education were selected. Departments of history and neurosciences will be selected to participate in both research and action projects.

Focused attempts to expand the professoriate and enrich the doctoral experience, by exposing more doctoral students to teaching opportunities beyond their own campuses, have paralleled these two projects. Guided by leadership at the CGS and the Association of American Colleges and Universities (AAC&U), the Preparing Future Faculty initiative involved hundreds of students and several dozen schools. The program assumed that "for too many individuals, developing the capacity for teaching and learning about fundamental professional concepts and principles remain accidental occurrences. We can—and should—do a better job of building the faculty the nation's colleges and universities need."[15] In light of recent surveys and studies, the Preparing Future Faculty program is quickly becoming the Preparing Future Professionals program, modeled on programs started at Arizona State University, Virginia Tech, University of Texas, and other universities.

Mention should also be made of the Graduate Education Initiative funded by the Andrew W. Mellon Foundation. Between 1990 and 2000, this program gave "approximately $80 million to assist students in 52 departments at 10 leading research universities. These departments were encouraged to review their curricula, examinations, advising, official timetables, and dissertation requirements to facilitate timely degree completion and to reduce attrition, while maintaining or increasing the quality of doctoral training they provided."[16] Although this project will be carefully evaluated, the evaluation has yet to be completed since some of the students have yet to graduate.

---

[11]The National Association of Graduate and Professional Students (2000).

[12]The 14 participating universities were: University of Colorado, Boulder; University of California, Irvine; University of Michigan; University of Pennsylvania; University of Washington; University of Wisconsin, Madison; University of Texas, Austin; Arizona State University; Duke University; Howard University; Indiana University; Princeton University; Washington University, St. Louis; and Yale University.

[13]See, http://www.woodrow.org/responsivephd/initiative.html.

---

[14]LaPidus (2000).

[15]Gaff, et al. (2000:x).

[16]Zuckerman and Meisel (2000).

ASSESSMENT OF DOCTORAL PROGRAMS AND ITS RELATION TO CALLS FOR REFORM

The calls for reform in doctoral education, although confirmed by testimony, surveys of graduate deans, and student surveys, do not have a strong underpinning in systematic data collection. With the exception of a study by Golde and Dore, which covered 4,000 students in a limited number of fields and institutions, and another by Cerny and Nerad, who investigated outcomes in 5 fields and 71 institutions, there has been little study at the national level of what doctoral programs provide for their students or of what outcomes they experience after graduation. National data gathering, which must, of necessity, be conducted as part of an assessment of doctoral programs, provides an opportunity for just such an investigation.

To date, the calls for reform agree that doctoral education in the United States remains robust, that it is valued at home and abroad, but that it must change if we are to remain an international leader. There is no commonly held view of what should and can be reformed. At the moment there is a variety of both research and action projects. Where agreement exists it centers on the need for versatile doctoral programs; on a greater sense of what students expect, receive, and value; on emphasizing the need to know, publicize, and control time to degree and degree completion rates as well as on the conclusion that a student's assessment of a program should play a role in the evaluation of that program.

This conclusion points to the possibility that a national assessment of doctoral education can contribute to an understanding of practices and outcomes that goes well beyond the attempts to assess the effectiveness of doctoral education undertaken in past NRC studies. The exploration of this possibility provided a major challenge to this Committee and presented the promise that, given a solid methodology, the next study could provide an empirical basis for the understanding of reforms in doctoral education.

PLAN OF THE REPORT

The previous sections present a picture of the broader context in which the Committee to Examine the Methodology of Assessing Research-Doctorate Programs approached its work. The rest of the report describes how the Committee went about its task and what conclusions it reached concerning fields to be included in the next study, quantitative measures of the correlates of quality, measures of student educational processes and outcomes, the measurement of scholarly reputation and how to present data about it, and the general conclusion about whether a new study should be undertaken.

2

How the Study Was Conducted

LAYING THE GROUNDWORK

In many ways, the completion of the 1995 Study led immediately into the study of the methodology for the next one. In the period between October of 1995, when the 1995 assessment was released, and 1999, when a planning meeting for the current study was held, *Change* magazine published an issue containing two articles on the NRC rankings—one by Webster and Skinner (1996) and another by Ehrenberg and Hurst (1996). In 1997, Hugh Graham and Nancy Diamond argued in their book, *The Rise of American Research Universities*, that standard methods of assessing institutional performance, including the NRC assessments, obscured the dynamics of institutional improvement because of the importance of size in determining reputation. In the June 1999 *Chronicle of Higher Education*,[1] the criticism was expanded to include questioning the ability of raters to perform their task in a scholarly world that is increasingly specialized and often interdisciplinary. They recommended that in its next study the NRC should list ratings of programs alphabetically and give key quantitative indicators equal prominence alongside the reputational indicators.

The taxonomy of the study was also immediately controversial. The study itself mentioned the difficulty of defining fields for the biological sciences and the problems that some institutions had with the final taxonomy. The 1995 taxonomy left out research programs in schools of agriculture altogether. The coverage of programs in the basic biomedical sciences that were housed in medical schools was also spotty. A planning meeting to consider a separate study for the agricultural sciences was held in 1996, but when funding could not be found, it was decided to wait until the next large assessment to include these fields.

Analytical studies were also conducted by a number of scholars to examine the relationship between quantitative and qualitative reputational measures.[2] These studies found a strong statistical correlation between the reputational measures of scholarly quality of faculty and many of the quantitative measures for all the selected programs.

The Planning Meeting for the next study was held in June of 1999. Its agenda and participants are shown in Appendix C. As part of the background for that meeting, all the institutions that participated in the 1995 Study were invited to comment and suggest ways to improve the NRC assessment. There was general agreement among meeting participants and institutional commentators that a statement of purpose was needed for the next study that would identify both the intended users and the uses of the study. Other suggested changes were to:

- Attack the question of identifying interdisciplinary and emerging fields and revisit the taxonomy for the biological sciences,
- Make an effort to measure educational process and outcomes directly,
- Recognize that the mission of many programs went beyond training Ph.D.s to take up academic positions,
- Provide quantitative measures that recognize differences by field in measures of merit,
- Analyze how program size influences reputation,
- Emphasize a rating scheme rather than numerical rankings, and
- Validate the collected data.

In the summer following the Planning Meeting, the presidents of the Conference Board of Associated Research Coun-

---

[1]Graham and Diamond (1999:B6).

[2]Two examples of these studies were: Ehrenberg and Hurst (1998) and Junn and Brooks (2000).

15

cils and the presidents of three organizations, representing graduate schools and research universities,[3] met and discussed whether another assessment of research-doctorate programs should be conducted. Objections to doing a study arose from the view that graduate education was a highly complex enterprise and that rankings could only oversimplify that complexity; however, there was general agreement that, if the study were to be conducted again, a careful examination of the methodology should be undertaken first. The following statement of purpose for an assessment study was drafted:

> The purpose of an assessment is to provide common data, collected under common definitions, which permit comparisons among doctoral programs. Such comparisons assist funders and university administrators in program evaluation and are useful to students in graduate program selection. They also provide evidence to external constituencies that graduate programs value excellence and assist in efforts to assess it. More fundamentally, the study provides an opportunity to document how doctoral education has changed but how important it remains to our society and economy.

The next 2 years were spent discussing the value of the methodology study with potential funders and refining its aims through interactions with foundations, university administrators and faculty, and government agencies. A list of those consulted is provided in Appendix B. A teleconference about statistical issues was held in September 2000,[4] and it concluded with a recommendation that the next assessment study include careful work on the analytic issues that had not been addressed in the 1995 Study. These issues included:

- Investigating ways of data presentation that would not overemphasize small differences in average ratings.
- Gaining better understanding of the correlates of reputation.
- Exploring the effect of providing additional information to raters.
- Increasing the amount of quantitative data included in the study so as to make it more useful to researchers.

A useful study had been prepared for the 2000 teleconference by Jane Junn and Rachelle Brooks, who were assisting the Association of American Universities' (AAU) project on Assessing Quality of University Education and Research. The study analyzed a number of quantitative measures related to reputational measures. Junn and Brooks made recommendations for methodological explorations in the next NRC study with suggestions for secondary analysis of data from the 1995 Study, including the following:

- Faculty should be asked about a smaller number of programs (less than 50).
- Respondents should rate departments 1) in the area or subfield they consider to be their own specialization and then 2) separately for that department as a whole.
- The study should consider using an electronic method of administration rather than a paper-and-pencil survey.[5]

Another useful critique was provided in a position paper for the National Association of State Universities and Land Grant Colleges by Joan Lorden and Lawrence Martin[6] that resulted from the summer 1999 meeting of the Council on Research Policy and Graduate Education. This paper recommended that:

- Rating be emphasized, not reputational ranking,
- Broad categories be used in ratings,
- *Per capita* measures of faculty productivity be given more prominence and that the number of measures be expanded,
- Educational effectiveness be measured directly by data on the placement of program graduates and a "graduate's own assessment of their educational experiences five years out."

THE STUDY ITSELF

The Committee to Examine the Methodology for the Assessment of Research-Doctorate Programs of the NRC held its first meeting in April 2002. Chaired by Professor Jeremiah Ostriker, the Committee decided to conduct its work by forming four panels whose membership would consist of both committee members and nonmembers who could supplement the committee's expertise.[7] The panels were comprised of both committee members and outside experts and their tasks were the following:

[3]These were: John D'Arms, president, American Council of Learned Societies; Stanley Ikenberry, president, American Council on Education; Craig Calhoun, president, Social Science Research Council; and William Wulf, vice-president, National Research Council. They were joined by: Jules LaPidus, president, Council of Graduate Schools; Nils Hasselmo, president, Association of American Universities; and Peter McGrath, president, National Association of State Universities and Land Grant Colleges.

[4]Participants were: Jonathan Cole, Columbia University; Steven Fienberg, Carnegie-Mellon University; Jane Junn, Rutgers University; Donald Rubin, Harvard University; Robert Solow, Massachusetts Institute of Technology; Rachelle Brooks and John Vaughn, Association of American Universities; Harriet Zuckerman, Mellon Foundation; and NRC staff.

[5]*Op. cit.*, p. 5.
[6]Lorden and Martin (n.d.).
[7]Committee and Panel membership is shown in Appendix A.

Panel on Taxonomy and Interdisciplinarity

This panel was given the task of examining the taxonomies that have been used in past studies, identifying fields that should be incorporated into the study, and determining ways to describe programs across the spectrum of academic institutions. It attempted to incorporate interdisciplinary programs and emerging fields into the study. Its specific tasks were to:

- Develop criteria to include/exclude fields.
- Determine ways to recognize subfields within major fields.
- Identify faculty associated with a program.
- Determine issues that are specific to broad fields: agricultural sciences; biological sciences; arts and humanities; social and behavioral sciences; physical sciences, mathematics, and engineering.
- Identify interdisciplinary fields.
- Identify emerging fields and determine how much information should be included.
- Decide on how fields with a small number of degrees and programs could be aggregated.

Panel on the Review of Quantitative Measures

The task of this panel was to identify measures of scholarly productivity, educational environment, and characteristics of students and faculty. In addition, it explored effective methods for data collection. The following issues were also addressed:

- Identification of scholarly productivity measures using publication and citation data, and the fields for which the measures are appropriate.
- Identification of measures that relate scholarly productivity to research funding data, and the investigation of sources for these data.
- Appropriate use of data on fellowships, awards, and honors.
- Appropriate measures of research infrastructure, such as space, library facilities, and computing facilities.
- Collection and uses of demographic data on faculty and students.
- Characteristics of the graduate educational environment, such as graduate student support, completion rates, time to degree, and attrition.
- Measures of scholarly productivity in the arts and humanities.
- Other quantitative measures and new data sources.

Panel on Student Processes and Outcomes

This panel investigated possible measures of student outcomes and the environment of graduate education. Questions addressed were:

- What quantitative data can be collected or are already available on student outcomes?
- What cohorts should be surveyed for information on student outcomes?
- What kinds of qualitative data can be collected from students currently in doctoral programs?
- Can currently used surveys on educational process and environment be adapted to this study?
- What privacy issues might affect data gathering? Could institutions legally provide information on recent graduates?
- How should a sample population for a survey be identified?
- What measures might be developed to characterize participation in postdoctoral research programs?

Panel on Reputational Measures and Data Presentation

This panel focused on:

- A critique of the method for measuring reputation used in the past study.
- An examination of alternative ways for measuring scholarly reputation.
- The type of preliminary data that should be collected from institutions and programs that would be the most helpful for linking with other data sources (e.g., citation data) in the compilation of the quantitative measures.
- The possible incorporation of industrial, governmental, and international respondents into a reputational assessment measure.

In the process of its investigation the panel was to address issues such as:

- The halo effect.
- The advantage of large programs and the more prominent use of per capita measures.
- The extent of rater knowledge about programs.
- Alternative ways to obtain reputational measures.
- Accounting for institutional mission.

All panels met twice. At their first meetings, they addressed their charge and developed tentative recommendations for consideration by the full committee. Following committee discussion, the recommendations were revised. The Panel on Quantitative Measures and the Panel on Student Processes and Outcomes developed questionnaires that were fielded in pilot trials. The Panel on Reputational Measures and Data Presentation developed new statistical techniques for presenting data and made suggestions to conduct matrix sampling on reputational measures, in which different raters would receive different amounts of information about the programs they were rating. The Panel on Taxonomy developed a list of fields and subfields and reviewed input from scholarly societies and from those who responded to several versions of a draft taxonomy that were posted on the Web.

TABLE 2-1 Characteristics for Selected Universities.

	Univ. of Southern California	Florida State Univ.	Yale Univ.	Univ. of Maryland	Michigan State Univ.	Univ. of Wisconsin-Milwaukee	Rensselaer Polytechnic Institute	Univ of California-San Francisco
Location	Los Angeles, CA	Tallahassee, FL	New Haven, CT	College Park, MD	East Lansing, MI	Milwaukee, WI	Troy, NY	San Francisco, CA
Year of Foundation	1880	1851	1701	1856	1855	1885	1824	1873
Graduate Enrollment (Year)	9,088 (1998-99)	6,383 (Fall 2001)	n/a	9,061 (Fall 2001)	7,752 (Fall 2001)	4,099 (2000)	2,003	2,578
Number of Schools	18	17	10	13	15	11	5	6
Doctoral Degree Programs	71	72	73	68	79	17	25	16
Total Ph.D.s (Year: 2000)	411	261	325	460	429	77	92	81
Total S&E Ph.D.s (Year: 2000)	265	112	216	319	278	43	83	64
Number of Graduate Faculty*	2,398	1,015	3,125	3,069	1,988	773	357	n/a
Type of Institution	Private	Land Grant	Private (Ivy League)	Land Grant	Land Grant	Small (local)	Private	State

Source: Peterson's Graduate & Professional Programs: An Overview, 1999, 33rd edition, Princeton, NJ.
NOTE: In the actual study, these data would be provided and verified by the institutions themselves.

Pilot Testing

Eight institutions volunteered to serve as pilot sites for experimental data collection. Since the purpose of the pilot trials was to test the feasibility of obtaining answers to draft questionnaires, the pilot sites were chosen to be as different as possible with respect to size, control, regional location, and whether they were specialized in particular areas of study (engineering in the case of RPI, biosciences in the case of UCSF). The sites and their major characteristics are shown in Table 2-1.

Coordinators at the pilot sites then worked with their offices of institutional research and their department chairs to review the questionnaires and provide feedback to the NRC staff, who, in turn, revised the questionnaires. The pilot sites then administered them.[8]

Questionnaires for faculty and students were placed on the Web. Respondents were contacted by e-mail and provided individual passwords in order to access their questionnaires. Institutional and program questionnaires were also available on the Web. Answers to the questionnaires were immediately downloaded into a database. Although there were glitches in the process (e.g., we learned that whenever the e-mail subject line was blank, our messages were discarded as spam), generally speaking, it worked well. Web-administered questionnaires could work, but special follow-up attention[9] is critical to ensure adequate response rates (over 70 percent).

Data and observations from the pilot sites were shared with the committee and used to inform its recommendations, which are reported in the following four chapters. Relevant findings from the pilot trials are reported in the appropriate chapters.

---

[8]Two of the pilot sites, Yale University and University of California-San Francisco, provided feedback on the questionnaires but did not participate in their actual administration.

[9]In the proposed study, the names of non-respondents will be sent to the graduate dean, who will assist the NRC in encouraging responses. Time needs to be allowed for such efforts.

3

Taxonomy

In any assessment of doctoral programs, a key question is: Which programs should be included? The task of constructing a taxonomy of programs is to provide a framework for the analysis of research-doctorate programs as they exist today, with an eye to the future. A secondary question is: Which fields should be grouped together and what names should be given to these aggregations?

CRITERIA FOR INCLUSION

The construction of a taxonomy inevitably confronts limitations and requires execution of somewhat arbitrary decisions. The proposed taxonomy builds upon the previous studies, in order to represent the continuity of doctoral research and training and to provide a basis for potential users of the proposed analysis to identify information important to them. Those users include scholars, students, academic administrators as well as industrial and governmental employers. Furthermore, a taxonomy must correspond as much as possible to the actual programmatic organization of doctoral studies. In addition, however, a taxonomy must capture the development of new and diversifying activity. Thus, it is especially true in the area of taxonomy that the recommendations that follow should be taken as advisory rather than binding by the committee that is appointed to conduct the whole study. These efforts are further complicated by the frequent disparity among institutional nomenclatures, representing essentially the same research and training activities, as well as by the rise of interdisciplinary work. The Committee did its best to construct a taxonomy that reflected the way most graduate programs are organized in most research universities but realizes that there may be areas where the fit may not be perfect. Thus, the subject should remain open to review by the next committee.

We recognize that scholarship and research in interdisciplinary fields have grown significantly since the last study. Some of this work is multidisciplinary; some is cross-disciplinary or interdisciplinary.[1] We could not devise a single standard for all possible combinations. Where possible, we have attempted to include acknowledged interdisciplinary fields such as Neuroscience, Biomedical Engineering, and American Studies. In other instances, we listed areas as emerging fields. Our goal remains to identify and evaluate inter-, multi-, and cross-disciplinary fields. Once they become established scholarly areas and meet the threshold for inclusion in the study established by this and future committees, they will be added to the list of surveyed fields.

The initial basis for the Committee's consideration of its taxonomy was the classification of fields used in the Doctorate Records File (DRF), which is maintained by the National Science Foundation (NSF) as lead agency for a consortium that includes the National Institutes of Health, U.S. Department of Agriculture, National Endowment for the Humanities, and U.S. Department of Education.[2] Based on these data, the Committee reviewed the fields included in the 1995 Study to determine whether new fields had grown enough to merit inclusion and whether the criteria themselves were sensible. In earlier studies, the criteria for inclusion had been that a field must have produced at least 500 Ph.D.s over the most recent 5 years and be offered by programs that had produced 5 or more Ph.D.s in the last 5 years in at least 25 universities. After reviewing these criteria, the Committee agreed that the field inclusion criterion should be kept, although a few fields in the humanities should continue to be included even though they no longer met the threshold requirement.

---

[1] By "multidisciplinary" or "cross-disciplinary" research we mean research that brings together scholars from different fields to work on a common problem. In contrast, interdisciplinary research occurs when the fields themselves are changed to incorporate perspectives and approaches from other fields.

[2] National Science Foundation (2002).

Recommendation 3.1: The quantitative criterion for inclusion of a field used in the preceding study should be, for the most part, retained—i.e., 500 degrees granted in the last 5 years.

The Committee also reviewed the threshold level for inclusion of an individual program and, given the growth in the average size of programs, generally felt that a modification was warranted. A minimal amount of activity is required to evaluate a program.

This parameter is modified from the previous study—3 degrees in 3 years—to account for variations in small fields. The 25-university threshold is retained.

Recommendation 3.2: Only those programs that have produced 5 or more Ph.D.s in the last 5 years should be evaluated.

Two fields in the humanities, Classics and German language and literature, had been included in earlier studies but have since fallen below the threshold size for inclusion in terms of Ph.D. production. Adequate numbers of faculty remain, however, to assess the scholarly quality of programs. In the interests of continuity with earlier studies and the historical importance of these fields, the Committee felt that they should still be included. Continuity is a particularly important consideration. In the biological sciences, where the Committee redefined fields, the fields themselves had changed in a way that could not be ignored. Smaller fields in the humanities have a different problem. A number of them are experiencing shrinking enrollments, but it can be argued that inclusion in the NRC study may assist the higher-quality programs to survive.

Recommendation 3.3: Some fields should be included that do not meet the quantitative criteria, if they were included in earlier studies.

The number of degrees awarded in a field is determined by the number of new Ph.D.s who chose that field from the Survey of Earned Doctorates based on the NSF taxonomy. However, there is no external validation that these fields correctly reflect the current organization of doctorate programs. The Committee sought to investigate this question by requesting input from a large number of scholarly and professional societies (see Appendix B). Beginning in December 2002, the proposed taxonomy was also presented in a public Website and suggestions were invited. As of mid-June 2003, over 100 suggestions had been received, and both the taxonomy and the list of subfields were discussed with the relevant scholarly societies. The taxonomy was also used in the pilot trials, and although the correspondence was not exact, the pilot sites found a reasonable fit with their graduate programs. This taxonomy included new fields that had grown or been overlooked in the last study. It also reflected

the continuing reorganization of the biological sciences. The taxonomy put forward by the Committee, compared with the taxonomy for the 1995 Study, appears in Table 3-1.

Inclusion of the arts and sciences and engineering fields preserves continuity with previous studies. Inclusion of agriculture recognizes the increasing convergence of research in those fields with research in the traditional biological sciences and the legitimacy of the research in these fields, separate and independent of other traditional biological disciplines.

The biological sciences presented special problems. The past decade has seen an expansion of research and doctoral training in the basic biomedical sciences. However, these Ph.D. programs are not all within faculties of arts and sciences, which was the focus of the 1995 Study. Many of them are located in medical schools and were overlooked in earlier studies. The Committee sought input from basic biomedical science programs in medical schools through the Graduate Research Education and Teaching Group of the American Association of Medical Colleges to assure systematic inclusion the next time the study is conducted.

Recommendation 3.4: The proposed study should add research-doctorate programs in agriculture to the fields in engineering and the arts and sciences that have been assessed in the past. In addition, it should make a special effort to include programs in the basic biomedical sciences that are housed in medical schools.

The Committee reviewed doctorate production over the period 1998-2002 for fields included in the Doctorate Records Field. It identified those fields that had grown beyond the size threshold, notably communication, theatre research, and American studies. In addition, it reviewed the organization of life sciences fields and expanded them somewhat, reflecting changes in doctoral production and the changing nature of study. These decisions by the Committee, as mentioned at the beginning of the chapter, should not be viewed as binding by the committee appointed to conduct the full study.

Recommendation 3.5: The number of fields should be increased, from 41 to 57.

A number of additional programs in applied fields urged that they be included in the study. The Committee decided not to include those fields for which much research is directed toward the improvement of practice. These fields include social work, public policy, nursing, public health, business, architecture, criminology, kinesiology, and education. This exclusion is not intended to imply that high-quality research is not conducted in these fields. Rather, in those areas in which research is properly devoted to improving practice, evaluation of such research requires a more nuanced approach than evaluation of scholarly reputation

TABLE 3-1 Taxonomy Comparison—1995 Study and Current Committee

Major Fields

1995 Taxonomy	2005 Taxonomy
Biological Sciences	**Life Sciences**
Biochemistry and Molecular Biology	Biochemistry, Biophysics, and Structural Biology
	Molecular Biology
Cell and Developmental Biology	Developmental Biology
	Cell Biology
Ecology, Evolution, and Behavior	Ecology and Evolutionary Biology
	Microbiology
Molecular and General Genetics	Genetics, Genomics, and Bioinformatics
	Immunology and Infectious Disease
Neurosciences	Neuroscience and Neurobiology
Pharmacology	Pharmacology, Toxicology, and Environmental Health
Physiology	Physiology
	Plant Sciences
	Food Science and Food Engineering
	Nutrition
	Entomology
	Animal Sciences
	Emerging Fields
	Biotechnology
	Systems Biology
Engineering	**Physical Sciences, Mathematics, and Engineering**
Aerospace Engineering	Aerospace Engineering
Biomedical Engineering	Biomedical Engineering
	Biological and Agricultural Engineering
Chemical Engineering	Chemical Engineering
Civil Engineering	Civil and Environmental Engineering
Electrical Engineering	Electrical and Computer Engineering
Industrial Engineering	Operations Research, Systems Engineering, and Industrial Engineering
Materials Science	Materials Science and Engineering
Mechanical Engineering	Mechanical Engineering
Physical Sciences	
Astrophysics and Astronomy	Astrophysics and Astronomy
Chemistry	Chemistry
Computer Science	Computer and Information Science
Geosciences	Earth Sciences
Mathematics	Mathematics
	Applied Mathematics
Oceanography	Oceanography, Atmospheric Sciences, and Metereology
Physics	Physics
Statistics/Biostatistics	Statistics and Probability
	Emerging Fields
	Nanoscience and Nanotechnology
	Information Science

continues

TABLE 3-1 Contiunued

Major Fields	
1995 Taxonomy	**2005 Taxonomy**
Arts and Humanities	**Arts and Humanities**
	American Studies
Art History	History of Art, Architecture, and Archaeology
Classics	Classics
Comparative Literature	Comparative Literature
English Language and Literature	English Language and Literature
French Language and Literature	French Language and Literature
German Language and Literature	German Language and Literature
(History listed under Social and Behavioral Sciences)	History
Linguistics	*(Linguistics listed under Social and Behavioral Sciences)*
Music	Music
Philosophy	Philosophy
Religion	Religion
Spanish Language and Literature	Spanish and Portuguese Language and Literature
	Theatre and Performance Studies
	Global Area Studies
	Emerging Fields:
	Race, Ethnicity, and Post-Colonial Studies
	Feminist, Gender, and Sexuality Studies
	Film Studies
Social and Behavioral Sciences	**Social and Behavioral Sciences**
Anthropology	Anthropology
	Communication
Economics	Economics
	Agricultural and Resource Economics
Geography	Geography
History	*(History listed under Arts and Humanities)*
(Linguistics listed under Arts and Humanities)	Linguistics
Political Science	Political Science
Psychology	Psychology
Sociology	Sociology
	Emerging Field
	Science and Technology Studies

alone. It should also include measures of the effectiveness of the application of research. The Committee's view is that this task is beyond the capacity of the current or proposed methodology. It does recommend that, if these fields can achieve a consensus on how to measure the quality of research, the NRC should consider including such measures in future studies.

The question can also be raised: Are the additional costs in both respondent and committee time of increasing the number of fields by 37 percent justified? To answer this question, it is useful to consider the benefits of the increase. First, the Committee believes that the current taxonomy reflects the classification of doctoral programs as they exist today. The Committee felt it was better to increase the number of fields through an expanded taxonomy than to force institutions to shape themselves to the Procrustean bed of an outmoded one. Second, the Committee was convinced

that newly included large programs, such as communication, could benefit from having the quality of scholarship in their programs assessed by peer reviewers and that such information, as well as data describing the programs, could assist potential students who are making a selection among many programs. Third, the agricultural sciences are an area in which important and fundamental research occurs. They were excluded from earlier studies primarily because the focus of those studies was the traditional arts and sciences fields. Today, they are changing and are increasingly similar to the applied biological sciences. In addition, they are an important part of land-grant colleges and universities, an important sector of graduate education. On the cost side, the expense of gathering and analyzing data has fallen impressively as information technology has improved. The primary additional direct cost of increasing the number of fields is the cost of assuring adequate response rates.

NAMING ISSUES

The Committee wanted its taxonomy to be forward-looking and to recognize evident trends in the organization of knowledge. One such example is the growth in inter-disciplinary research. This trend should be reflected in the study in a number of ways: the naming of broad fields, flexibility in the number of programs to which a faculty member may claim affiliation, and the recognition of emerging fields.

The Committee recognized that activities in engineering and the physical sciences are converging in many respects.

Recommendation 3.6: The fields should be organized into four major groupings rather than the five in the previous NRC study. Mathematics and Physical Sciences are merged into one major group along with Engineering.

As discussed above, the Committee urges that the agricultural sciences be included in future studies, because of their focus on basic biological processes in agricultural applications and the importance of the research and doctorates in these fields, separate and independent of other traditional biological disciplines. This leads to the more inclusive name of "life sciences" for the group of fields that includes both the agricultural and biological sciences.

Recommendation 3.7: Biological Sciences, one of the four major groupings, should be renamed "Life Sciences."

The question of naming arises in all fields. Graduate program names vary by university, depending on when the program was established and what the area of research was called at that time. The Committee agreed that programs and faculty need some guidance, given a set of program names, as to where to place themselves. This can be accomplished through the inclusion of subfield names in the taxonomy. Subfield names identify areas of specialization within a field. They are not all-inclusive but will allow students, faculty, and evaluators to recognize and identify the specific activities of complex fields. Programs in the subfields themselves will not be ranked individually. They will, however, permit the identification of "niche" as opposed to general programs for the purpose of subsequent analysis. The Committee obtained the names of subfields through consultation with scholarly societies, by requesting subfield titles on the project Webpage, and through inquiries sent out to faculty. These subfields are listed in Appendix E.

Recommendation 3.8: Subfields should be listed for many of the fields.

Some programs will find that the taxonomy fits, but others may find that they have separate programs for a number of subfields, or conversely, have programs that contain two or more fields. The Committee recognized that these sorts of problems will arise and asks that programs try to fit themselves into the taxonomy. This will help assure comparability across programs. For example, a physics program may also contain an astrophysics subspecialty. This program should list its physics faculty as one "program" for the purposes of ratings and list its astrophysics faculty as another, separate program, even though the two are not, in fact, administratively separate. Programs that combine separate fields listed in the taxonomy will be asked to indicate this in their questionnaires and the final tables will report that the fields are part of a combined program. A task left to the next committee is to assure that the detailed questionnaire instructions will permit both accurate assignment of faculty to research fields and accurate descriptions of programs available to students.

The flip side of this problem arises in the agricultural sciences. Many institutions have separate programs for each subfield. Their faculty lists should contain faculty names from all the programs, rather than separate listings for each program. These conventions, although somewhat arbitrary, make it possible to include faculty from programs that would otherwise be too small to rate. In all cases, faculty should then identify their subfields on the faculty questionnaire. This would permit analysis of the effect of rater subfield on ratings.

FINDINGS FROM THE PILOT TRIALS

Six of the pilot sites got to the point of administering the questionnaires and attempting to place their programs within the draft taxonomy. The taxonomy proved generally satisfactory for all the broad fields except for the life sciences. A particular problem was found with "molecular biology." It was pointed out that molecular biology is a tool that is widely used across the life sciences but is not a specific graduate program. The same is true, to a lesser extent, for cell biology. Given the trial taxonomy, many biological science programs are highly interdisciplinary and combine a number of fields. The Committee hopes to address this issue by asking respondents to indicate if faculty, who specialize in a particular field, teach and supervise dissertations in a broad biological science graduate program.

Another problem was that the subfield listing was viewed as "dated." The Committee addressed this finding by querying colleagues at their own and other institutions and by asking scholarly societies. This is an issue, however, that should be revisited prior to the full study.

EMERGING FIELDS

The upcoming study must attempt to identify the emergence of new fields that may develop and qualify as separate fields in the future. It should also assess fields that have emerged in the past decade. For purposes of assessment, these fields present two problems. First, although an area of study exists in many universities, it may or may not have its own doctoral program. Cinema studies, for example, may be taught in a separate program or it may exist in graduate programs in English, Theatre, or Communication, among others. To present data only about separate and named programs gives a misleading idea of the area of graduate study. Second, the emerging areas of study may be transitory. Computational biology, for example, is just beginning to exist. It may become a broad field that will, in the future, include genomics, proteomics, and bioinformatics, or, alternatively, it may be incorporated into yet another field. The Committee agreed that the existence of these fields should be recognized in the study but that they were either too new or too amorphous to identify a set of faculty for reputational comparison of programs. Quantitative data should be collected about them to assist in possible evaluation in future studies.

Recommendation 3.9: Emerging fields should be identified, based on their increased scholarly and training activity (e.g., race, ethnicity, and Post-Colonial studies; feminist, gender, and sexuality studies; nanoscience;

computational biology). **The number of programs and degrees, however, is insufficient to warrant full-scale evaluation at this time. Where possible, they should be included as subfields. In other cases, they should be listed separately.**

Finally, the Committee was perplexed about what to do about the fields of area studies that focus on different parts of the world. These fields are highly interdisciplinary and draw on faculty across the university. By themselves, they are too small to be included, yet they are likely to be of growing importance as trends toward a global economy and its accompanying stresses continue. The Committee decided to create a broad field, "Global Area Studies," in the Arts and Humanities and to list each area as a subfield within this heading.

Recommendation 3.10: A new broad field, "Global Area Studies," should be included in the taxonomy and include as subfields: Near Eastern, East Asian, South Asian, Latin American, African, and Slavic Studies.

4

Quantitative Measures

This chapter proposes and describes the quantitative measures relevant to the assessment of research-doctorate programs. These measures are valuable because they

- Permit comparisons across programs,
- Allow analyses of the correlates of the qualitative reputational measure,
- Provide potential students with a variety of dimensions along which to compare program characteristics, and
- Are easily updateable so that, even if assessing reputation is an expensive and time-intensive process, updated quantitative measures will allow current comparisons of programs.

Of course, quantitative measures can be subject to distortion just as reputational measures can be. An example would be a high citation count generated by a faulty result, but these distortions are different from and may be more easily identified and corrected than those involving reputational measures. Each quantitative measure reflects a dimension of the quality of a program, while reputational measures are more holistic and reflect the weighting of a variety of factors depending on rater preferences.

The Panel on Quantitative Measures recommended to the Committee several new data-collection approaches to address concerns about the 1995 Study. Evidence from individuals and organizations that corresponded with the Committee and the reactions to the previous study both show that the proposed study needs to provide information to potential students concerning the credentials required for admission to programs and the context within which graduate education occurs at each institution. It is important to present evidence on educational conditions for students as well as data on faculty quality. Data on post-Ph.D. plans are collected by the National Science Foundation and, although inadequate for those biological sciences in which post-doctoral study is expected to follow the receipt of a degree, they do differentiate among programs in other fields and

should be reported in this context. It is also important to collect data to provide a quantitative basis for the assessment of scholarly work in the graduate programs.

With these purposes in mind, the Panel focused on quantitative data that could be obtained from four different groups of respondents in universities that are involved in doctoral education:

University-wide. These data reflect resources available to, and characteristics of, doctoral education at the university level. Examples include: library resources, health care, child care, on-campus housing, laboratory space (by program), and interdisciplinary centers.

Program-specific. These data describe the characteristics of program faculty and students. Examples include: characteristics of students offered admission, information on program selectivity, support available to students, completion rates, time to degree, and demographic characteristics of faculty.

Faculty-related. These data cover the disciplinary sub-field, doctoral program connections, Ph.D. institution, and prior employment for each faculty member as well as tenure status and rank.

Currently enrolled students. These data cover professional development, career plans and guidance, research productivity, research infrastructure, and demographic characteristics for students who have been admitted to candidacy in selected fields.

In addition to these data, which would be collected through surveys, data on research funding, citations, publications, and awards would be gathered from awarding agencies and the Institute for Scientific Information (ISI), as was done in the 1995 Study.

The mechanics of collecting these data have been greatly simplified since 1993 by the development of questionnaires and datasets that can be made available on the Web as well as software that permits easy analysis of large datasets. This technology makes it possible to expand the pool of potential raters of doctoral programs.

MEASURABLE CHARACTERISTICS OF DOCTORAL PROGRAMS

The 1995 Study presented data on 17 characteristics of doctoral programs and their students beyond reputational measures. These are shown in Table 4-1. Although these measures are interesting and useful, it is now possible to gather data that will paint a far more nuanced picture of doctoral programs. Indicators of what data would be especially useful have been pointed out in a number of recent discussions and surveys of doctoral education.

Institutional Variables

In the 1995 Study, data were presented on size, type of control, level of research and development funding, size of the graduate school, and library characteristics (total volumes and serials). These variables paint a general picture of the environment in which a doctoral program exists. Does it reside in a big research university? Does the graduate school loom large in its overall educational mission? The Committee added to these measures that were specifically related to doctoral education. Does the institution contribute to health care for doctoral students and their families? Does it provide graduate student housing? Are day care facilities provided on campus? All these variables are relevant to the quality of life of the doctoral student, who is often married and subsisting on a limited stipend.

The Committee took an especially hard look at the quantitative measures of library resources. The number of books and serials is not an adequate measure in the electronic age. Many universities participate in library consortia and digital material is a growing portion of their acquisitions. The Committee revised the library measures by asking for budget data on print serials, electronic serials, and other electronic media as well as for the size of library staff.

An addition to the institutional data collection effort is the question about laboratory space. Although this is a program characteristic, information about laboratory space is provided to the National Science Foundation and to government auditors at the institutional level. This is a measure of considerable interest for the laboratory sciences and engineering, and the Committee agreed that it should be collected as a possible correlate of quality.

Program Characteristics

The 1995 Study included data about faculty, students, and graduates gathered through institutional coordinators, Insti-

tute for Scientific Information (ISI) and the NSF Doctorate Records File (DRF). For the humanities, it gathered data on honors and awards from the granting organizations. Most of the institutional coordinators did a conscientious and thorough job, but the Committee believes that it would be helpful to pursue a more complex data-collection strategy that would include a program data collector (usually the director of graduate studies) in addition to the key institutional coordinator, a questionnaire to faculty, and questionnaires to students in selected programs. This approach was tested with the help of the pilot institutions. The institutional coordinator sent the NRC e-mail addresses of respondents for each program. The NRC then provided the respondent a password and the Web address of the program questionnaire. A similar procedure was followed for faculty whose names were provided by the program respondents. Copies of the questionnaires may be found in Appendix D.

In 1995, programs were asked for the number of faculty engaged in doctoral education and the percentage of faculty who were full professors. They were also asked for the numbers of Ph.D.s granted in the previous 3 years, their graduate enrollment both full-time and part-time, and the percentage of females in their total enrollment. Data on doctoral recipients, such as time to degree and demographic characteristics, came entirely from the DRF and represented only those who had completed their degrees.

The Committee believed that more informative data could be collected directly from the program respondents. Following the 1995 Study, a number of questions had been raised about the DRF data on time to degree. More generally, the Committee observed that data on graduates alone gave a possibly biased picture of the composition and funding of students enrolled in the program. The program questionnaire contains questions that are directly relevant to these concerns.

In the area of faculty characteristics, the program questionnaire requests the name, e-mail address, rank, tenure status, and demographic characteristics (gender, race/ethnicity, and citizenship status) of each faculty member associated with the program. Student data requested include characteristics of students offered admission, information on program selectivity, support available to students, completion rates, and time to degree. It also asks whether the program requires a master's degree prior to admission to the doctoral program, since this is a crucial consideration affecting the measurement of time to degree. The questionnaire also permits construction of a detailed profile of the percentage of students receiving financial aid and the nature of that aid. Finally, the questionnaire asks a variety of questions related to program support of doctoral education: whether student teaching is mentored, whether students are provided with their own workspaces, whether professional development is encouraged through travel grants, and whether excellence in the mentoring of graduate students by faculty is rewarded. These are all "yes/no" questions that impose little respondent burden.

TABLE 4-1 Data Recommended for Inclusion in the Next Assessment of Research-Doctorate Programs. Bolded Elements Were Not Collected for the 1995 Study.

Institutional Characteristics

Variable	Description
Year of First Ph.D.	*The year in which the Doctorate Records File (DRF) first recorded a Ph.D. Since the DRF information dates back only to 1920, institutions awarding Ph.D.s prior to 1920 were identified by other sources, such as university catalogs or direct inquiries to the institutions. Because of historic limitations to this file, this variable should be considered a general indicator not an institutional record.*
Control	*Type of "Institutional Control": PR=private institution; PU=public institution.*
Enrollment Total	*Total full- and part-time students enrolled in Fall 2003 in courses creditable toward a diploma.*
Graduate	*Full- and part-time students in Fall 2003 in nonprofessional programs seeking a graduate degree.*
Total R&D	*Average annual expenditure for research and development at the institution for the previous 5 years in constant dollars.*
Federal R&D	*Average annual federal expenditure for research and development at the institution for the previous 5 years in constant dollars.*
Professional Library Staff	*Number of library staff (FTE).*
Total Library Expenditures	*Total library expenditure of funds from regular institutional budgets and other sources, such as research grants, special projects, gifts, endowments, and fees for services for the previous academic year.*
Library Expenditures: Acquisition of Books	*Total library expenditure of funds for book acquisition from regular institutional budgets and other sources, such as research grants, special projects, gifts, endowments, and fees for services for the previous academic year.*
Library Expenditures: Print Serials	*Total library expenditure of funds for print serials from regular institutional budgets and other sources, such as research grants, special projects, gifts, endowments, and fees for services for the previous academic year.*
Library Expenditures: Electronic Serials	*Total library expenditure of funds for serials in electronic media from regular institutional budgets and other sources, such as research grants, special projects, gifts, endowments, and fees for services for the previous academic year.*
Library Expenditures: Microprint and Electronic Databases	*Total library expenditure of funds for microprint and electronic databases from regular institutional budgets and other sources, such as research grants, special projects, gifts, endowments, and fees for services for the previous academic year.*
Health Care Insurance	*Whether health care insurance is available to enrolled doctoral students under an institutional plan. Whether and for whom (TAs, RAs, all) percentage of premium cost is covered.*
Childcare Facilities	*Available to graduate students? Subsidized? Listings made available?*
University-Subsidized Student Housing	*Available to doctoral students?*
University Awards/ Recognition	*Teaching or research by doctoral students? Mentoring of doctoral students by faculty?*
University-Level Support for Doctoral Students	*Available for travel to professional meetings? For research off-campus? Available to help students improve their teaching skills? Placement assistance? Available for travel to professional meetings? Available to help students improve their teaching skills? Placement assistance?*

Doctoral Program Characteristics

Variable	Description
Total Students	*The number of full- and part-time graduate students enrolled in the Fall of the survey year.*
Student Characteristics	*Numbers, full-time and part-time status, gender, race/ethnicity, citizenship status.*
Ph.D. Production	*Numbers of Ph.D.s awarded in each of the previous 5 years.*
Program Median Time to Degree	*Year by which half the entering cohort had completed, averaged over five cohorts. For programs for which half never complete, the percentage completing within 7 years.*
Master's Required	*Whether the program requires completion of a master's degree prior to admission.*
Financial Support	*Proportion of first-year students who receive full support. Number of years for which students may expect full financial support (including Fellowships, RAships, and TAships). Whether summer support is available. Percent receiving externally funded support. Percent receiving university-funded support.*

continues

TABLE 4-1 Data Recommended for Inclusion in the Next Assessment of Research-Doctorate Programs.
Bold elements were not collected for the 1995 Study.

Doctoral Program Characteristics (continued)

Variable	*Description*
Teaching Assistant Work Load	*Average number of courses per term that a TA is expected to teach.*
Individually Assigned Student Workspace	*For all students? For TAs? For RAs?*
GRE Scores	*Whether GRE is required for admission. Average and minimum verbal and quantitative scores.*
Number of Acceptances	*Number of applicants who are accepted into the program for the past 3 years.*
Number Who Enroll	*Number of accepted students who enroll in the program for the past 3 years.*
Awards for Teaching/ Research, Faculty Mentoring	*Whether the program gives awards for graduate student teaching/research or for faculty mentoring of doctoral students.*
Program Support for Student Travel to Meetings	*Whether the program provides some form of travel support for doctoral students to attend professional meetings.*
Teaching Skill Support	*Whether there is an organized program to help doctoral students improve their teaching skills.*
Laboratory Space	*For each doctoral program in science and engineering, the number of net available square feet of laboratory space in the previous academic year. Also, an indication of whether this space is shared with other doctoral programs.*
Related Interdisciplinary Centers	*Listing of centers in which program doctoral students may carry out research.*
Data Collection on Student Outcomes	*Whether the program collects such data. Whether it makes data available to potential students.*
Competitor Programs	*List of up to five programs with which the program normally competes for graduate students.*
Post-doctoral Plans by Type of Employer	*Obtained from the NSF Survey of Doctoral Recipients, the percentage of Ph.D.s over the previous 5 years by type of employer.*

Program Faculty

Variable	*Description*
Total Faculty	*Total number of faculty participating in the program (teaching or supervising dissertations).*
Faculty Characteristics	*Rank, tenure status, gender, race/ethnicity, citizenship status, years since Ph.D., time at this institution.*
Percent Full	*Percentage of full professors participating in the program.*
Percent Support	*Percentage of program faculty with research support (1999-2003).*
Percent Engaged in More than One Doctoral Program	*Percentage of program faculty who teach graduate courses or supervise dissertations in other programs.*
Number of Awards[a]	*Total number of awards and honors attributed to program faculty for the period 1999-2003.*
Awarded Faculty[a]	*Percentage of program faculty that have received at least one honor or award for the period 1999-2003.*
Percent Publications[b]	*Percentage of program faculty (total faculty) publishing in the period 1999-2003.*
Publications/Faculty[b]	*The ratio of the total number of program publications in the period 1999-2003 to the number of program faculty (total faculty).*
Citations/Faculty[b]	*The ratio of the total number of program citations in the period 1999-2003 to the number of program faculty (total faculty).*
Faculty Characteristics	*Listing by name and e-mail address of faculty who are affiliated with the program through either teaching or supervision of dissertations. Rank, tenure status, whether US citizen/permanent resident, gender, race/ethnicity, date and year of highest degree.*

[a]For Arts and Humanities.

[b]For the fields in Engineering and the Sciences. Arts and Humanities may be included, depending on whether adequate book and monograph citations and publication sources exist.

Faculty Characteristics

In the 1995 Study, a brief faculty questionnaire was administered to the raters who produced the reputational rankings. These raters were drawn from a sample of faculty nominated by their institutional coordinators. The sample size reflected the number of programs in each field. The brief questionnaire asked raters the year, institution, and date of their highest degree as well as their current field of specialization. The Committee believes that the faculty questionnaire should be modified to collect certain other data. For example, the university origins of current faculty are a direct measure of which graduate programs are training Ph.D.s who become faculty at research universities. Data on date of degree would also permit a comparison of origins of recently hired faculty as compared to faculty hired, for example, more than 20 years ago. Although subfield data were collected for the 1995 Study, they were not used. They could be useful in improving program descriptions for potential graduate students and for assuring that specialist programs are rated by knowledgeable peers in the same specialty.

The Committee also believes that additional questions asked of faculty could permit a richer description of interdisciplinarity. For example, faculty could list all programs in which they have participated, either by teaching or serving on dissertation committees. Many faculty would be listed as members of more than one graduate program, and for the purposes of the reputational survey, the Committee recommends that they be listed as program faculty for *all* programs with which they are associated. To avoid the possibility of double counting the output of productive faculty, objective measures should be attributed *pro rata* among the various programs in which they are listed. The decision as to how to prorate an effort should be made by the faculty member with guidance that they should try to describe how time devoted to doctoral education (teaching and student mentoring) has been allocated among the programs for the past 3-year period.

The Committee was concerned that programs might want to associate a well-known faculty member with as many programs as possible in order to boost its rating, even if he or she were not involved with the program. Allocation of publications should serve to discourage this behavior.

Student Characteristics and Views

Student observations have not been a part of past assessments of research-doctorate programs. Past studies have included data about demographic characteristics and about sources of financial support of Ph.D. recipients drawn from the DRF and about graduate student enrollment collected from the doctoral institutions. Another student measure was "educational effectiveness of the doctoral program," and for reasons discussed in Chapter 6, the Committee is recommending the elimination of this measure. The approach for measuring student processes and outcomes is discussed in Chapter 5.

PILOT TRIAL FINDINGS

The pilot trials were conducted over a 3-month period. The most important finding was that 3 months was barely sufficient for dealing with the study questionnaires. The full study should probably allow at least 4-6 months for data submission. The answers to many of the questions are prepared for other data collection efforts, but additional time is needed to customize answers to fit the taxonomy and to permit time for follow-up with nonrespondents.

All institutions carried out the trial through a single point of contact for the campus. This single point of contact worked with institutional research offices and program contacts to answer questions as well as interacted with NRC staff to assure that data definitions were uniform.

Electronic data collection worked well for institutions, programs, and faculty. We learned that it was better not to provide a hard copy alternative (as contrasted to Web response), since hard copy data simply had to be re-entered in databases once it was received by the NRC. All the pilot institutions store and access institutional and program data electronically. E-mail is the standard mode of communication with faculty and the rates of faculty response (60 percent) were high for a one-wave administration.

The Committee also learned that more precise definitions are needed to guide respondents. For example, when asking for data about "first-year doctoral students" a distinction may be needed about whether the students have a master's in the field. Care needs to be taken not to include terminal master's students, and precise definitions of "full-time" and "part-time" should be included.

The Committee learned the following from the questionnaire responses:

Institutional Questionnaire.
- Library expenditures: Not all institutions separate e-media expenditures from print expenditures.
- Space: The questionnaire needs to provide guidance about how to allocate shared space. Answers to space questions also depend on how well the institution's programs fit the taxonomy. If the fit is poor, the allocation of space is arbitrary.
- Graduate student awards and support are more appropriately queried at the program level.

Program questionnaire.
- Programs had difficulty filling out the inception cohort matrix but believed they could have done it if they had had more lead time.
- Programs knew who their competitors were for doctoral students.

• Programs that required GREs knew the averages and minima. For programs that do not require GREs, it would be helpful to ask what percentage of applicants submit GRE scores as well as report averages and minima only for those programs that are above a certain level (e.g., 80 percent).

• Requests for faculty lists and faculty data should be separate from requests for other program data.

Faculty questionnaire.

• E-mail notifications must have a sufficiently informative subject heading so that they are not mistaken for spam.

• Questionnaires should contain a due date.

• Faculty associated with more than one program should be asked to fill out only one questionnaire. The NRC needs to develop procedures to duplicate information for the other programs with which a faculty member is associated.

• Some faculty identified their program by a name other than that of the program that submitted their name. A procedure must be developed to resolve this problem.

Each pilot institution was asked to provide comments on the questionnaires. These comments, some of which are reported above, will be used as background material for the committee that conducts the full study. Draft questionnaires for the full study should be reviewed by a number of institutional researchers from a diverse set of institutions as well as by survey researchers.

Data Collected from Other Sources

The Committee recommends that most of the quantitative data presented in the 1995 Study from other sources be collected again. These include: publication and citation data from ISI, data on research grants from government agencies and large private foundations, data on books from the Arts and Humanities Citation Index, and data on awards and honors from a large set of foundations and professional societies. Student data from the Doctorate Record File should be considered for inclusion but checked for inconsistencies against institutional and program records. In the case of inconsistencies, a validation process should be designed.

RECOMMENDATIONS

The Committee recommends that the data listed in Bold type in Table 4-1 be added to the quantitative measures that were collected for the 1995 Study.

5

Student Education and Outcomes

INTRODUCTION

The 1995 Study contained a reputational measure that assessed the "Effectiveness of [the] Program in Educating Research Scholars/Scientists"[1] but was quite straightforward in stating, "Reputational ratings do not tell us how well a program is structured, whether it offers a nurturing environment for students, or if the job placement experiences of its graduates are satisfactory."[2] Yet all of these attributes are important to the quality of a doctoral education. Despite the known shortcomings of "E," the reputational measure of educational effectiveness, the 1995 Study proceeded to measure it in order to maintain continuity with the previous 1982 Study.

The Committee observed the high degree of correlation between "Q," the reputational measure of scholarly quality of faculty, and "E," and asked the Panel on Student Processes and Outcomes to focus on defining direct measures that could be obtained from programs or through surveys that would provide information about the education of doctoral students that was comparable across programs and at the same time useful to potential students and to program administrators. It constructed surveys for first-year students, for mid-course students, and for graduates who had completed their programs 5-7 years before. These questionnaires are shown in Appendix D.

When it came to the point of administering the questionnaires, however, the method of questioning students and graduates directly about their programs ran into a number of obstacles. Prior to the pilot trials, the pilot coordinators warned the Committee about the low response rates often encountered when administering questionnaires to graduate students.[3] Raising these response rates was costly and time-

consuming. The Committee viewed this as a very serious problem, since the comparisons of programs, which lie at the heart of the assessment, require valid data from each program. If response rates were low, there would be a problem in deciding whether responses were coming from a biased sample. Finding addresses for graduates is also time-consuming. Thus, after considerable debate, the Committee decided to pilot only a questionnaire for mid-course students in selected fields.

This chapter reports on what the Committee agreed it would like to measure that would be valuable in assessing the effectiveness of doctorate programs and on the results of its pilot trials in five fields. It recommends that a survey of admitted-to-candidacy students be conducted as part of the full study for a limited number of fields. It also discusses two other questionnaires, one for first-year students and one for graduates who are 5-7 years beyond completion, which may be helpful to programs that want to survey their own students and graduates.

GUIDING PRINCIPLES

Student input is important in improving doctoral education. Direct assessment of student experiences provides information about program effectiveness that cannot be obtained by other means.

Although faculty are key in the education of research-doctoral students, the effectiveness of that education may hinge on student perceptions and reactions. Interviews with doctoral students conducted by Jody Nyquist and her colleagues[4] were confirmed by a survey of doctoral students in 11 selected fields at 27 universities conducted by Golde and Dore (2001), who found that graduate students did not believe that the training they received was preparing them

---

[1]Goldberger et al., eds. (1995:119-125).
[2]*Op. cit.* p. 23.
[3]For example, Golde and Dore (2001) had a 42 percent response rate.

[4]Nyquist et al. (1999).

for the jobs that they were likely to take and "Many students do not clearly understand what doctoral study entails, how the process works and how to navigate it effectively."[5] The Committee agreed that effective doctoral programs should have formal means to obtain student input in order to improve their effectiveness.

A student survey can provide a statistical description of students in a program, information about practices in that program, and assist future students in the selection of graduate programs.

Data about graduate programs can be collected from program administrators (see Table 4-1) and also from students. Students can report reliably on what they have experienced in their doctoral programs. Programs can report on what they offer, the overall characteristics of their students, and what information they collect about student outcomes. Such data should permit prospective students to distinguish among programs. If there are differences among programs in the extent to which students have received training in particular areas, a report on these differences will permit potential students to match what a program offers to what they desire in a program.

Information on educational outcomes is essential in assessing the quality and effectiveness of doctoral programs.

It should be no surprise that doctoral education is preparatory to employment. Traditionally, the Ph.D. is certification that a degree holder can conduct original research. Fifty years ago, most doctorate degree holders became academic researchers. This is no longer the case. In fact, in almost all fields, fewer than half of new Ph.D. recipients are employed as tenure-track faculty in research universities.[6] In recognition of this change, the 1995 Committee on Science, Engineering, and Public Policy (COSEPUP) study, *Reshaping the Graduate Education of Scientists and Engineers* recommended that

> Academic departments should provide employment information and career advice to prospective and current students in a timely manner and should help students see career choices as a series of branching decisions. Students should be encouraged to consider discrete alternative pathways when they have met their qualifying requirements.[7]

A corollary of this recommendation is that prospective students should know what kind of employment recent program graduates have undertaken. The Association of American Universities (AAU) reiterated this recommendation in 1998.[8] Yet these data are still not routinely available from doctoral programs. This is in contrast to other components of graduate education, for example professional schools, in which employment outcomes are routinely publicized and used as a recruitment tool.

The collection and presentation of data on employment outcomes of graduates neither requires nor implies a hierarchy of employment outcomes for Ph.D.s. Rather, a prospective doctoral student who wants to become employed as a teacher at a liberal arts college or a researcher in an industrial laboratory should be able to learn whether the programs under consideration have produced graduates who work in such settings and provide appropriate training in those directions. Moreover, data suggest that many graduates are employed in sectors other than those that they sought at the outset of their graduate studies.[9] Programs that provide opportunities for students to explore career options and encourage exploration through formal and informal means are more likely to create an environment that is supportive of student choices and which prepares students for opportunities in varying labor markets.

Given these guiding principles, the Panel developed three questionnaires that would collect the information recommended in a number of recent reports designed to improve the quality of doctoral education. Only one of these was actually pilot tested, but all three questionnaires are discussed below and provided in the appendices in the hope that they may be adopted and implemented by interested institutions and professional societies.

INFORMATION FROM STUDENTS

The questions for students were designed with the intention of collecting data that are comparable across programs. Thus, they are limited primarily to factual questions about what the student was informed of, exposed to, or experienced with respect to teaching, research, and professional development. Other questionnaires have asked students how they felt about or evaluated aspects of their experience.[10] The Committee rejected this approach as being beyond the scope of the present study, although the approach would be informative about student attitudes.

Questions for First-Year Students

The proposed questionnaire is shown in Appendix D. These questions focus on information that the program provided the student either in the application process or following admission. They ask whether students were provided information prior to attending about:

---

[5]Golde and Dore (2001).
[6]Nerad and Cerny (2002) and Nerad and Cerny (1999).
[7]COSEPUP (1995:86).
[8]AAU Committee on Graduate Education (1998).

---

[9]NSF (2001).
[10]Examples include Golde and Dore, *op. cit.,* and the National Doctoral Program Survey fielded by the National Association of Graduate and Professional Students in 1999.

- Program costs and financial aid,
- Career prospects in the field,
- Program time to degree,
- Program requirements and expectations,
- Rates of program completion,
- Employment of recent graduates.

Questions are also asked about whether a program provided a formal orientation program as the student began his or her studies, about career goals or previous participation in post-baccalaureate education, and the status of financial support.

The Committee decided not to field this questionnaire, in part because the pilot trials were carried out toward the end of the academic year, when it was impractical to obtain satisfactory response rates in a short period of time. For the full study, the Committee believes that the benefit from information gathered through this questionnaire would probably not justify the cost of administration. However, it has included the questionnaire in Appendix D in the event that universities might want to use it to compare program practices across programs or if consortia of universities wish to use it for comparative purposes.

Questions for Students Who Are "Mid-Program" Students

This questionnaire is shown in Appendix D. It is intended for registered students who have finished their course work and preliminary examinations and are in the process of completing their dissertation, a status frequently referred to as "advanced-to-candidacy." This status is reached at varying times in different disciplines but generally means that a student who has entered a program without a relevant master's degree will have been in a program for at least 2 years and, thus, is definitely a doctoral student. The decision as to which group of students are in "mid-course" and should receive the questionnaire will vary by field and program.

Questions are grouped into three categories:

1. Educational Program

These questions deal with whether the student is expected to earn a master's degree as part of his/her training and whether the doctoral program is part of a joint degree program. Also addressed are the student's career goals upon entry into a program and whether these have changed as well as queries about the student's three largest sources of support.

2. Program Characteristics

Questions in this category address the kinds of professional skills in which the student received instruction (e.g., presentation skills, proposal writing, preparing articles for publication, working in teams, independent research, project management, professional ethics, and speaking to nonacademic audiences); the kinds of teaching experiences to which the student was exposed and whether there was formal instruction and evaluation in teaching and an opportunity to teach in a variety of academic environments; the student's perception of the program environment (e.g., feedback, assessment of progress, career advice, mentoring, and liveliness of the intellectual climate); the availability of infrastructure (e.g., personal workspace, and computing facilities) and adequacy of library resources; student research productivity, research presentations, and any publications while enrolled in a doctoral program.

3. Student Demographic Information

These questions deal with the student's age, gender, citizenship, race/ethnicity, dependent care responsibilities, and level of parents' education.

Questions for Graduates 5-7 Years Out

This questionnaire was not pilot tested because the pilot site coordinators told us that they would not be able to provide us with mail or e-mail addresses for their graduates within the short time frame of 2-3 months. Cerny and Nerad[11] have been able to track down graduates 10-13 years after their degree at 61 research universities and achieved a response rate of over 60 percent. Programs that support students with institutional training grants from federal sources routinely track the employment of their graduates. Thus, we know that this is a possible task, although not necessarily a routine one, in all fields and institutions.

A more conceptual objection to using these data in an assessment of quality of current programs is that the program faculty and the curricula, which were in place 10 years before, may not be the same as are currently associated with the program. However, data on the career outcomes for graduates 5-7 years out can and should be collected by effective programs. NSF data report that the 5-7 year period allows Ph.D. recipients, including those with post-doctoral appointments, to settle into more stable employment than the position they entered into immediately after graduation. Collection of such data permits programs to understand what type of positions their graduates are taking and to consider whether their curricular offerings provide adequate preparation for these positions. The Committee agreed that programs should track the career outcomes of their students until at least 5 years out and make this information available to prospective students. Such efforts would serve to indicate a positive sense of responsibility on the part of a program, demonstrating a desire to monitor program quality and effectiveness.

---

[11]See, for example, Nerad and Cerny (1999).

PILOT TRIAL FINDINGS

The pilot questionnaire for students admitted to candidacy was administered to 466 students from five fields at five institutions.[12] This was done in mid-April, which is late in the school year. A response rate of 25 percent was achieved with one follow-up mailing. When we inquired why the response rates were so low, we were told that it was late in the year and some students may have left campus. We were also told that many students do not access their university mailbox often. In earlier discussions, we had been told that the typical response rate during the middle of the school year is, at best, 40 percent. On the other hand, higher response rates (up to 80 percent) have been achieved when students and staff have been alerted in advance to the importance of the impending survey. The good news was that, for those who did answer the questionnaire, the items worked. All items were answered and we did not receive complaints about the items.

A 40 percent response rate would not be adequate for program-to-program comparisons. The Committee, however, decided that it should recommend a further trial, for five fields, as part of the full study. Questionnaires should be sent out early in the school year and programs should be asked to collect alternative e-mail addresses (in addition to the university mailbox) for their students.

CONCLUSIONS AND RECOMMENDATIONS

Having fielded a questionnaire for mid-course students with the pilot institutions, the Committee concluded that it would be feasible to conduct such a survey in a limited number of fields as part of an assessment of research-doctorate programs. The Committee also found, however, that institutions will need considerable lead time to be able to provide information on recent graduates. Whether a program collects such data is evidence of good practice. Thus, the Committee recommends:

Recommendation 5.1: The proposed NRC study of research-doctorate programs should conduct a survey of enrolled students in selected fields who have advanced to candidacy for the doctoral degree regarding their assessment of their educational experience, their research productivity, program practices, and institutional and program environment.

With respect to career outcomes of graduates, the committee recommends:

Recommendation 5.2: Universities should track the career outcomes of Ph.D. recipients both directly upon program completion and at least 5-7 years following degree completion in preparation for a future NRC doctoral assessment. A measure of whether a program carries out and publishes outcomes information for the benefit of prospective students and as a means of monitoring program effectiveness should be included in the next NRC assessment of research-doctorate programs.

---

[12]One institution sent the NRC e-mail addresses for an additional 411 students but did not indicate the field of their program. Questionnaires were not sent to these addresses.

6

Reputation and Data Presentation

INTRODUCTION

Since the first study of research-doctorate programs in 1925, users have focused on the reputational rating of programs as the primary measure for assessing the quality of doctoral programs. Even with the introduction of many quantitative measures in the 1982 and 1995 Studies, ratings of scholarly quality of faculty by other scholars in the same field and the resulting rankings of programs have remained the primary object of attention. Recognizing this fact, the Committee and its Panel on Reputational Measures and Data Presentation set as their task the development of procedures that would:

- Identify useful reputational measures,
- Select raters who have a knowledge of the programs that they are asked to rate,
- Provide raters with information about the programs they are rating, and
- Describe clearly the variation in ratings that result from a sample survey and present program ratings in a manner that meaningfully reflected this variation.

A useful reputational measure is one that reflects peer assessment of the scholarly quality of program faculty. Ideally, such a measure would be based only on the knowledge and familiarity of the raters with the scholarly quality of the faculty of the programs they are asked to rate and would not be directly influenced by other factors, such as the overall reputation of the program's institution (a "halo effect") or the size or age of the program. Both the 1982 and the 1995 Studies presented correlations of reputation with a number of other quantitative measures. The next assessment should expand on these correlational analyses and consider including and interpreting multivariate analyses.

An example of an expanded analysis that would be of considerable interest is one that explores the relation between scholarly reputation and program size. The 1982 Study found a linear relation between scholarly reputation of program faculty and the square root of program size. Ehrenberg and Hurst (1998) also found a positive effect of program size. Both these analyses suggest that there is a point beyond which an increase in program size ceases to be associated with a higher reputational rating, but it is also clear that small programs are not rated as high as middle and large size programs. Further analyses along these lines would be useful.

The Committee believes that the reputational measure of the scholarly quality of faculty is important and consequential. A highly reputed program may have an easier time attracting excellent students, good faculty, and research resources than a program that is less highly rated. At the same time, reputation is not everything. Students, faculty, and funders need to examine detailed program directions and offerings to be able to assess the quality of a program for their particular objectives.

THE MEASUREMENT OF SCHOLARLY QUALITY OF PROGRAM FACULTY: PRACTICES AND CRITICISMS

The Reputational Measure of Scholarly Quality of Program Faculty

To obtain the reputational measure of scholarly quality, raters have been presented with lists of faculty and the number of doctorates awarded in a program over the previous 5 years. They were then asked to rate the programs:

1. On a 3-point scale, their familiarity with the work of the program faculty,
2. On a 6-point scale, their view of the scholarly quality of program faculty (a seventh category was included—"Do not know well enough to evaluate").

For years, the use of a reputational survey to assess the scholarly quality of program faculty and the effectiveness of a doctoral program has attracted criticism. Critics cite program size as a factor that correlates with quality. The "halo effect" that raises the perceived quality of all programs in an institution that is considered to have a good reputation, the national visibility of a department or institution, and the "star effect" in which a few well-known faculty members in a program can also raise ratings. There are nonreputational measures by which individuals can assess programs, such as educational or research facilities and quality of graduate-level teaching and advising, but these are often not widely known outside the doctoral program, and raters would have limited information on which to make a judgment unless they are closely associated with it. In fact, the strong correlation between the reputational measure of scholarly quality of the program faculty ("Q") and the effectiveness of the doctoral program in training scholars ("E") present in past studies suggests that raters have little knowledge of educational programs independent from faculty lists.

Rater Selection

For the 1995 Study, a large enough number of raters was selected to provide 200 ratings for each program in non-biological fields and 300 ratings for biological science fields. For example, if there were 150 programs in a nonbiological field, then 600 raters would be needed to provide the 200 ratings, since each rater was asked to rate 50 programs. In the biological sciences the number of raters needed to rate 150 programs was 750, since 60 programs appeared on each questionnaire and 300 ratings was the desired goal. The reason for this increase in raters and ratings stems from the realization by the last study committee that their taxonomy did not accurately describe fields in the biological sciences and, therefore, the field of some raters did not often match that of the programs they were asked to rate.

Raters in the 1995 Study were selected in an almost random manner with the following restrictions: at least one rater was selected from each program; the number of raters from a particular program was proportional to the size of the program; and if there were more than three, raters were selected on the basis of faculty rank, with the first chosen from among a pool of full professors, the second from among associate professors, and so on. The response rate for this sample was about 50 percent across the 41 fields in the study, and in many cases the more visible national programs received most of the responses with about 100 ratings. Programs at regional universities received fewer ratings, and in some cases scores could not be averaged after trimming. It was also noted that, by using the question that asked for a rater's "familiarity" with the program faculty and by weighting the response to the question concerning program quality by familiarity, ratings increased for the higher-rated programs and decreased for lower-rated programs. It appears that more reliable and useable ratings would result if rater familiarity were considered.

Program Information

The last two assessments provided raters with a limited amount of program information. Faculty names by rank were listed on the questionnaire, and for some fields, the number of program graduates over a 5-year period was also included. This information was provided to assist raters in associating researchers with their institutions, but based on a sample of raters who were asked to indicate the number of names they recognized, most raters recognized at most one or two faculty members in most programs. Thus, it may have been that only the most visible scholars and scientists determine reputational rating and faculty lists may have been of little assistance in providing information to help raters. Additional program information or cues might assist raters in assessing program quality.

Variability of Reputational Measures

Since the National Surveys of Graduate Faculty for past studies were sample surveys, there is a certain amount of variability in the results. If a different sample of raters had been selected, the ratings would, in general, have been different.[1] This possible variability was described for past studies by estimating the confidence intervals for the scores of each program and displaying the results graphically to show the overlaps. However, this analysis was generally ignored by users and the rank order of the programs remained the focus of attention. An important remaining issue is the communication of uncertainty or variability of the ratings to users and the presentation of data that reflects the variability. Doing so can help to dispel a spurious impression of accuracy in ratings.

IS SCHOLARLY REPUTATION WORTH MEASURING?

While the 1995 Study has been criticized for many of the measures it reported, the major objection was its ranking of programs on the basis of scholarly reputation of program faculty. In particular, critics argued that few scholars know enough about more than a handful of programs in their discipline, that programs change more rapidly than the reputations that follow them, that response bias presents a false sense of program ratings, that reputation is dependent on program size, and that weak programs at well-known institutions benefit from a "halo effect." On the other hand, reputations of programs definitely exist for individual programs as well as universities. Reputational standing is real in its

---

[1]Cole and Cole (1973).

consequences and has a strong correlation with other indicators of quality. Perceptions of program quality held by knowledgeable outsiders is important to deans, department chairs, and other administrators in designing and promoting their programs; to governing boards in allocating resources across programs; and to prospective students in choosing among programs. More importantly, reputational measures provide a benchmark against which other quantitative measures can be calibrated.

The Panel on Reputational Measures and Data Presentation took the criticisms of the reputational measure as a challenge, recognizing that the techniques used in earlier studies to generate reputational ratings were developed in an era when there were fewer doctoral programs, program faculty were less specialized, and the mission of most doctoral programs was the training of students for academic positions. Although many doctorate holders were taking nonacademic jobs at the time of the 1995 Study, the desire to maintain continuity with earlier studies dictated a continuation of the earlier methodology. These changes in the doctoral education environment made the task of developing a meaningful reputational measure more difficult, but at the same time the technological developments of the past decade make possible the use of online questionnaires to enhance and expand the scope of a survey. Modern database analysis methods also provide users with techniques to analyze the results of reputational surveys as well as the quantitative measures from the study to address their program, institutional, and research needs.

ADDRESSING ISSUES RELATED TO REPUTATIONAL MEASURES

The issues to be addressed fell in two major categories: 1) the development of procedures that would improve the quality of a reputational survey, and 2) the presentation of data from the reputational survey that would minimize spurious inferences of precision in program ratings by users.

Efforts to improve the quality of reputational surveys focused on having a more informed rater pool by either providing raters with additional information about the programs they were rating or matching the characteristics of raters with those of the programs. Matching raters to programs appears to be a good idea, but it introduces many complications, since the variety of missions and subfields present in any one of the fields in the taxonomy would rapidly create a multidimensional stratification of the rater pool and introduce unknown biases. Developing a large rater pool with few constraints would provide ratings that could be analyzed on the basis of program and rater characteristics. This would enable a better understanding of the process that generates reputational ratings. It would also provide a sufficient number of ratings so that institutions could evaluate the study findings based on a sample of ratings they judge to be meaningful. For example, a program could analyze only those program ratings from raters at peer institutions. This would also allow institutions to analyze their programs with particular subfield specializations against those in other similarly specialized programs to gain a more accurate assessment. This could be done through the use of an online data-extraction program where there is a quantitative database for each program, and certain data, such as the list of program faculty, could be linked to the database to provide information on faculty productivity and scholarship.

Beyond the issue of survey methodology is the issue of data presentation for all the measures, reputational and quantitative, from the study. For the 1995 Study the data were collated into a large publication consisting primarily of statistical results—tables for each field displayed data for various measures. This will no longer be possible considering the increase in the number of measures, programs, and fields. For the 1995 Study a CD-ROM was also produced that contained the raw data from different data sources which were intended to serve as a research tool for specialized analyses. While this basic data set will be available for the next study in electronic form, there will also be a public-use file for general users to access, retrieve, and analyze any program included in the study. The printed study would provide examples of analyses that could be conducted using the data.

MODELS OF REPUTATION

Another criticism of the reputational measure of scholarly quality is that it ages between studies and, since the study is conducted only every 10 years or so, users must rely on an obsolete measure of reputation during the interim period. In fact, reputational ratings change very slowly over time, but users might find it helpful to be able to approximate the effects of program changes on their reputational status. One approach would be to construct a statistical model of reputation, dependent on quantitative variables. Using that model, it would then be possible to predict how the range of ratings would change when a quantitative variable changed, assuming the other variables remained constant. The parameters of such a model would measure the statistical effect of both the intrinsic and standardized quantitative variables on the mean of the reputational variable for all programs in a field. This would permit a program to estimate the effect on reputation of, for example, shortening time to degree or increasing the percentage of faculty with research funding. Examination of outliers in this estimation would permit the identification of those programs for which such a model "underpredicts" or "overpredicts" reputation. Programs experiencing a "halo effect" would have a better reputation than that predicted by the quantitative variables in the model alone. A technical description of such a model and examples of it using data from the 1995 Study are shown in Appendix G. Such a model could be used to estimate ratings during the period between studies, if programs updated their quantitative information regularly on a study Website.

However, there is a cautionary note for this type of analysis. It assumes that the relationships (the parameters) of the model are invariant over time. Only the values of the program characteristics change. If there is sufficient change in program characteristics for a field during the period between assessments, the assumption will not be valid. At this time it is not possible to judge the effects of time on the model or the soundness of this analysis, but when data are collected for the next assessment it will be possible to compare the model parameters in Appendix G with those estimated using new data on the same characteristics. The current analysis is also limited by the number of characteristics for which data was collected for the 1995 Study, and since the next assessment will collect data on more characteristics, the model might be improved with an expanded data set and further refinement through subsequent assessments.

FINDINGS AND RECOMMENDATIONS

Why Measure Scholarly Reputation at All?

The large amount of data collected during previous assessments of research-doctorate programs has been widely used and, in particular, scholarly reputation is a significant component of the evaluation of faculty and programs that has consequences for student choices, institutional investments, and resource acquisition. Reputation is one part of the "reality" of higher education that affects a tremendous number of decisions—where graduate students choose to study, where faculty choose to locate, and where resources may flow. It also has a strong correlation with honorific recognition of faculty. Critics have given reasons for discounting the reputational rating, including many that were stated earlier, but it is the most widely quoted and used statistic from the earlier studies, and by using better sampling methods and more accurate ways to present survey results it can be a more accurate and useful measure of the quality of research-doctorate programs. Institutions use the reputational measure to benchmark their programs against peer programs. If the measure were eliminated, institutions would no longer be able to map changes in programs in this admittedly ill-defined, but important, respect. The reputational measure also provides a metric against which program resources and characteristics can be compared, as similar quantitative measures for similar programs are compared across a large list of institutions. While students were not considered to be potential users of past studies, they, in fact, used the reputational ratings in conjunction with the other measures in the reports to select programs for graduate study. Future studies should encourage this use by students and provide both reputational and quantitative measures to assist them in their decisions.

The care taken by the NRC in conducting studies is another factor to consider with regard to the retention of the reputational measure. NRC studies are subjected to a rigorous review process, and the study committee would be primarily composed of academic faculty, university administrators, and others whose work involves the judgment of doctoral program quality. This may be the only reputational study of program quality that limits raters of programs to members of the discipline being rated. The proposed study will go even further to ensure that the ratings are made by people who know the programs that they rate. Further, unlike studies conducted by the popular press, NRC ratings are not based on weighted averages of factors. The reputational measure is a measure of evaluation of scholarly reputation of program faculty alone. Quantitative measures are presented unweighted. Thus users can apply the data from the study to reflect their own preferences, analyze the position of their own programs, and conduct their own comparisons. This cannot be accomplished with weighted measures.

Recommendation 6.1: The next NRC survey should include measures of scholarly reputation of programs based on the ratings by peer researchers in relevant fields of study.

Applying New Methods For Data Presentation

The presentation of average ratings in previous surveys has led to an emphasis on a single ordering of programs based on these average ratings and has given a spurious sense of precision to program rankings. Using a different set of raters would probably lead to a different set of average scores and a different rank ordering of programs. This is demonstrated by the confidence interval analyses that appeared in the last two NRC study reports. However, variance in the ratings and rankings implied by the confidence interval analysis did not translate into the way the ratings (calculated to two decimal places) were used. To show the variance in a more direct way, modern statistical methods of data display, based on resampling, can be used to show that there is actually a *range* of plausible ratings and, consequently, a range of plausible rankings for programs. These methods show that it is not unusual for these ranges to overlap, thereby dispelling the notion that a program is ranked precisely number 3, for example, but, rather, that it could have been ranked anywhere from first to fifth.

The question then arises: What is the best way to calculate statistically the range of uncertainty for a program? This presentation would go beyond presentation of the mean and standard error. The panel investigated two statistical methods— Random Halves and Bootstrap—to display the variability of results for a sample survey. These techniques are discussed technically in Appendix G.

The Random Halves method is a variation of the "Jack-knife Method," where only half of the ratings are used for each draw and there is no replacement. For the next draw, a different half of the whole sample is taken and a mean rating calculated for that half. Again, a mean rating would be produced for each program after each draw, and a range of ratings would result after a large number of samples. The interquartile rating range would then be presented as the program rating.

The Bootstrap method would be applied by taking a random draw from the pool of raters equal to the number of responses to the survey, then computing the mean rating and ranking for each program. This would be done "with replacement," i.e., a rater and the corresponding rating could be selected more than once. If this process were continued for a large number of draws, a range of ratings would be generated and a segment of that range for each program, such as the interquartile range, would be the range of possible ratings.

Both methods produce similar results if the number of samples taken is sufficiently large (greater than 50), since the variance of the average ratings for the two methods is nearly the same. It might be argued that neither method produces a true rating or ranking of a program by peers in the field, but unless the survey asked every person in the field to assess every program in the field and the response rate were 100 percent, the reputational rating would be subject to error. Presenting that error in a clear way would be helpful to users of the assessment.

An illustration of data presentation where the rankings are de-emphasized can be found in Chart 6-1A. The Random Halves method was applied using reputational survey data from the 1995 Study for programs in English Language and Literature. The data were resampled 100 times, and the programs were ordered alphabetically. Chart 6-1B is an example of the Bootstrap method applied to the same programs. Charts 6-2A and 6-2B present the same calculations for programs in mathematics. Tables 6-1 and 6-2 showing applications of Random Halves and Bootstrap methods can be found at the end of this chapter, following the charts.

The Committee favors the use of the Random Halves method over the Bootstrap Method, since it corresponds to surveying half the individuals in a rater pool and may be more intuitive to the users of the data. However either would be suitable. Both Random Halves, as a variation of the Jackknife Method, and Bootstrap are well-known in the statistics literature. Regardless of which technique is used, the interquartile range is then calculated in order to eliminate outliers. The results of either analysis could be presented in tabular or graphic form for programs listed alphabetically. These charts and tables are shown at the end of the chapter.

The use of either of these methods has the advantage of displaying variability in a manner similar to confidence interval computations in the past reports, without the technical assumption of a normal distribution of the data underlying the construction of a confidence interval. These methods provide ranges, rather than a single number, and differ from the presentation of survey results in the 1982 and 1995 Studies. The 1982 and 1995 Studies presented program rating as just one of the program characteristics in order to de-emphasize their importance. Tables in the1982 Study presented the data in alphabetical order by institution, and in the 1995 Study programs were ordered by faculty quality ratings. However, in both cases ratings were quickly converted into rankings by both the press and academic administrators, and programs were compared on that basis. If used properly, there is value in the use of rankings over ratings, since raters use subjective and different distributions of programs across the scale and this effect can only be eliminated by renormalization (or standardization). Rankings have the advantage of all nonparametric statistical measures—they are independent of variable and shifting rater scales. Thus the Committee concluded that if methods, such as Random Halves or Bootstrap, were used to address the issue of spurious accuracy, some of the defects attributed to misuse of rankings would be alleviated. The committee that will actually conduct the next assessment will have the option of presenting the data in an alphabetical order or rank order of a measure, such as the average faculty quality rating, or by the ranking range obtained from either the Bootstrap or Random Halves methods.

Recommendation 6.2: Resampling methods should be applied to ratings to give ranges of rankings for each program that reflect the variability of ratings by peer raters. The panel investigated two related methods, one based on Bootstrap resampling and another closely related method based on Random Halves, and found that either method would be appropriate.

The Use and Collection of Auxiliary Data

Previous reputational surveys have not helped our understanding of the causes and correlates of scholarly reputation. Raters were selected randomly and were asked to provide a limited amount of personal data. For the 1982 Study a simple analysis showed that raters rated programs higher if they had received their doctorate from that institution. Other information that could influence raters are the number of national conferences they attended in the last few years or their use of the Internet. These data might help to explain general questions of rater bias and the "halo effect." They may also be useful to programs and to university administrators in attempting to understand ratings and improve their programs.

New technologies such as Web-based surveys and matrix sampling allow us to add significant information on programs and on peer raters to allow better understanding of the causes and correlates of scholarly reputation. For example, statistical analyses could be conducted to relate rater characteristics to ratings. Beyond that, matrix sampling could be used to explore how ratings vary when raters are given information beyond just lists of faculty names.[2]

Recommendation 6.3: **The next study should have sufficient resources to collect and analyze auxiliary information from peer raters and the programs being rated to give meaning and context to the rating ranges that are obtained for the programs. Obtaining the resources to collect such data and to carry out such analyses should be a high priority.**

Survey Questions and Previous Survey

In the 1982 and 1995 assessments of research-doctorate programs three qualitative questions were asked of peer reviewers. These addressed the quality of the program faculty (Q), the effectiveness of the graduate program (E), and change in program quality in the past 5-year period (C). Only one question regarding the scholarly quality of the program faculty seemed to produce any significant results. The effectiveness question correlated highly with the quality question but did not appear to provide any other useful information. The results for the change question were also not significant, and the study committee in 1995 relied on a comparison of data and quality scores from the 1982 and 1995 Studies to analyze change in quality, in addition to change in program size and time to degree.

Recommendation 6.4: **The proposed survey should not use the two reputational questions on educational effectiveness (E) and change in program quality over the past 5 years (C). Information about changes in program quality can be found from comparisons with the previous survey, analyzed in the manner we propose for the next survey.**

The Selection of Peer Raters for Programs

Peer raters in a field were selected almost randomly, as described earlier, and only from the pool of faculty listed by the programs. Many Ph.D.s teach outside of research universities. While in some fields a large number of new Ph.D.s go into academic careers, this is far from universal. In many fields, such as those in engineering, a large number of doctorates go into industrial or governmental positions. How well the programs serve the needs of employers in these other areas has been a long-standing question. The 1995 Study investigated the possibility of surveying supervisors of

research teams or human resource officers to determine their opinions on academic programs, but the conclusion was that many companies hire regionally and there did not appear to be a way to integrate the information into a useful measure.

The issue of expanding the rater pool has not been resolved and various constituencies have asked that peer raters for programs be drawn from a wider pool than from the academic programs being rated. This could be assisted, in part, if the next committee included members who could represent industrial and governmental research, as well as academic institutions that are not research universities. The pool of raters could be expanded to include: industrial researchers in engineering; government researchers in fields such as physics, biomedical sciences, and mathematics; and faculty at 4-year colleges. It might be possible to identify a pool of raters from these sectors through nominations by professional organizations whose membership extends beyond academics.

Recommendation 6.5: **Expanding the pool of peer raters to include scholars and researchers employed outside of research universities should be investigated with the understanding that it may be useful and feasible only for particular fields.**

Consideration of Program Mission

Doctoral programs and institutions have varying missions and they serve different student populations and employment sectors. While large institutions have the capacity for programs that span many subfields of a discipline, smaller institutions may be limited to developing excellence in only one or two subfields. Comparison of broad programs to such "niche" programs would possibly be biased by the visibility of broader programs. Similarly, programs may have as their mission the training of researchers for regional industries and would, therefore, not have the same national prestige as programs whose graduates go into academic positions. One main criticism of past assessments was that these factors were not taken into account.

Taking subfield differences and program mission into consideration in the selection of raters for the reputational survey appears to be an obvious way to obtain more meaningful results. However, fragmenting rater pools into many segments based, for example, on subfields, would complicate the survey process by expanding the current 56 fields in the taxonomy to several hundred and many more, if factors such as the employment sectors of the graduates were considered. A more manageable way to account for program mission and other factors would be to have a sufficiently diverse rater pool and collect data on the raters and program characteristics so that individual programs could make comparisons with like programs on the basis of ratings from raters who have knowledge of those programs.

---

[2]Doing this would confuse "reputation" with more detailed knowledge of faculty productivity and other factors, but learning whether such information changes reputational ratings would be important to understanding what reputational measures actually tell us. This issue is discussed in greater detail below.

Recommendation 6.6: Ratings should not be conditioned on the mission of programs, but data to conduct such analyses should be made available to those interested in using them.

Providing Peer Raters with Additional Information

It is clear from the familiarity and visibility measures used for past studies that raters generally have little or no knowledge on which to base their rating for many programs. The limited amount of program information provided to raters in the last study may not have been of assistance, since many of the raters in the sample were unable to identify any faculty member in programs that were rated in the lower half of the rankings. It is therefore unclear on what basis many ratings were made. It is possible that information provided to raters could influence their ratings, especially for lower-rated programs, but this phenomenon is not well understood. Since the reputational survey for faculty will probably be Web-based, there is an opportunity to provide a large amount of quantitative data, such as the honors of individual faculty members or their publication information, directly in the questionnaire as links to a database. Exploring this approach for a sample of the programs and raters might provide insight in the use and value of reputational surveys.

Recommendation 6.7: Serious consideration should be given to the cues that are provided to peer raters. The possibility of embedding experiments using different sets of cues given to random subsets of peer raters should be seriously considered in order to increase the understanding of the effects of cues.

THE EFFECTS OF THE FAMILIARITY OF PEER RATERS WITH PROGRAMS ON THEIR RATINGS

It is well-known that raters who are more familiar with a program will rate it higher than raters who are less familiar. This fact was demonstrated by weighting the ratings with responses to the familiarity question for the 1995 Study; however, those results were actually not used in compiling the final ratings. In fact, the only familiarity measure that was used for that study was a visibility measure for each program that gave the percentage of raters who gave "Don't know well enough to evaluate" or "Little or no familiarity" as one or more of their responses to the five questions. By comparing this measure with the faculty quality measure it is clear that the more highly ranked programs were more visible. While accounting for familiarity in compiling program ratings may not change the ranking of programs, it does provide validity to ratings by assigning some basis for the rating.

Recommendation 6.8: Raters should be asked how familiar they are with the programs they rate and this information should be used both to measure the visibility of the programs and, possibly, to weight differentially the ratings of raters who are more familiar with the program.

Chart 6-1A: Interquartile Range of Program Rankings* in English Language and Literature—Random Halves

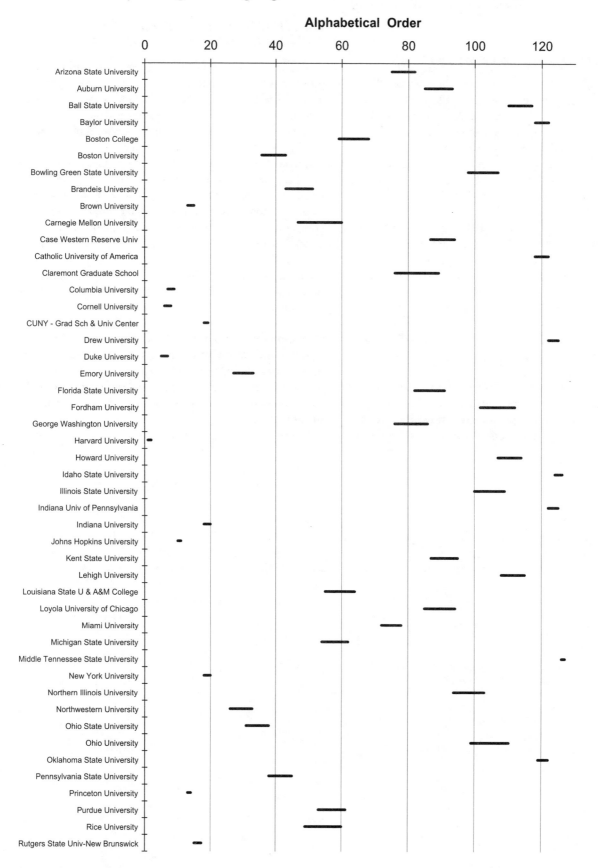

Chart 6-1A: Interquartile Range of Program Rankings* in English Language and Literature—Random Halves (Cont.)

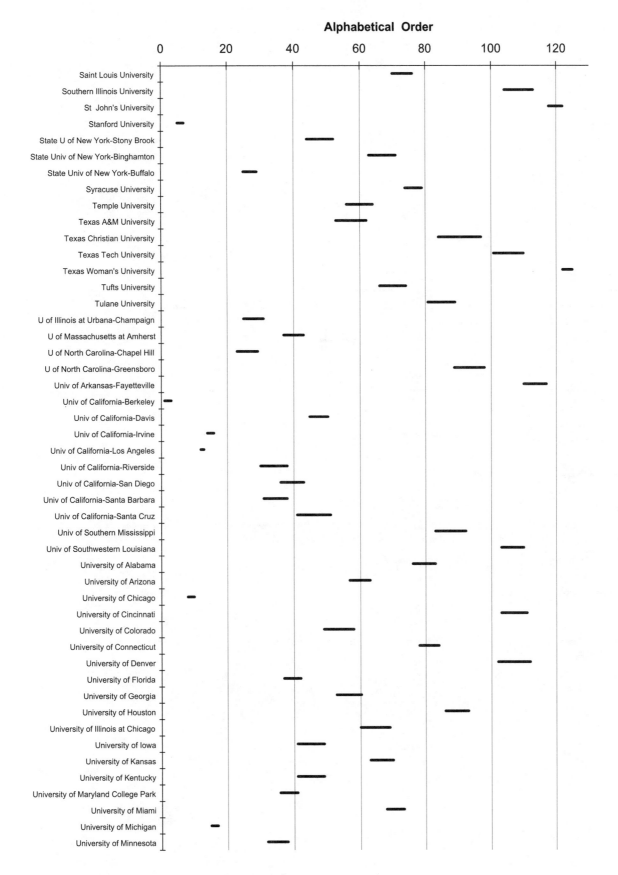

Chart 6-1A: Interquartile Range of Program Rankings* in English Language and Literature—Random Halves (Cont.)

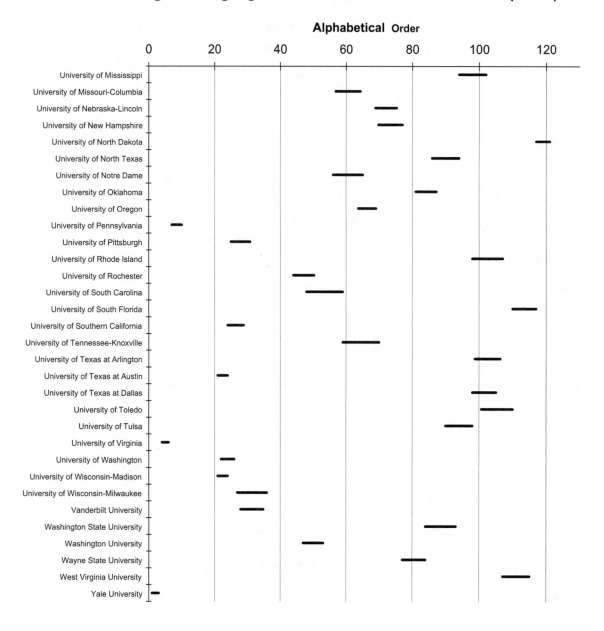

*Data from 1995 Study.

Chart 6-1B: Interquartile Range of Program Rankings* in English Language and Literature—Bootstrap

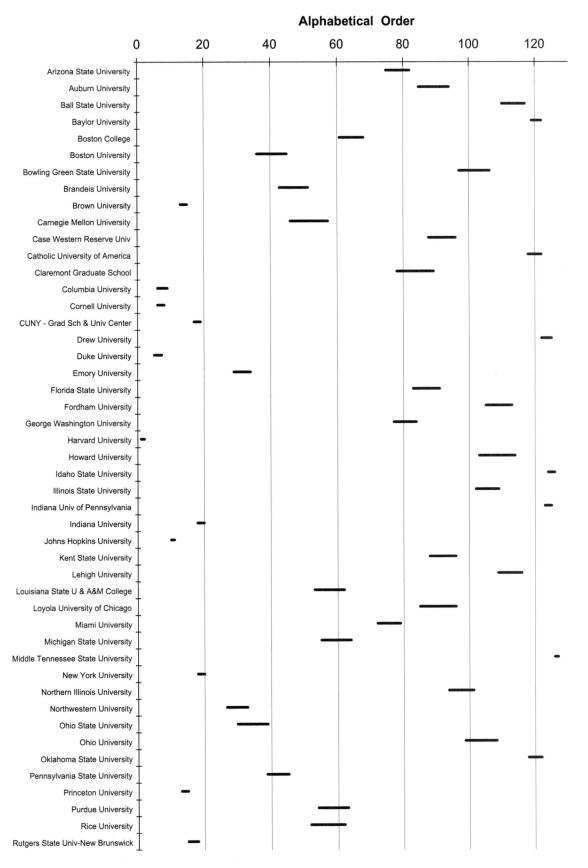

Chart 6-1B: Interquartile Range of Program Rankings* in English Language and Literature—Bootstrap (Cont.)

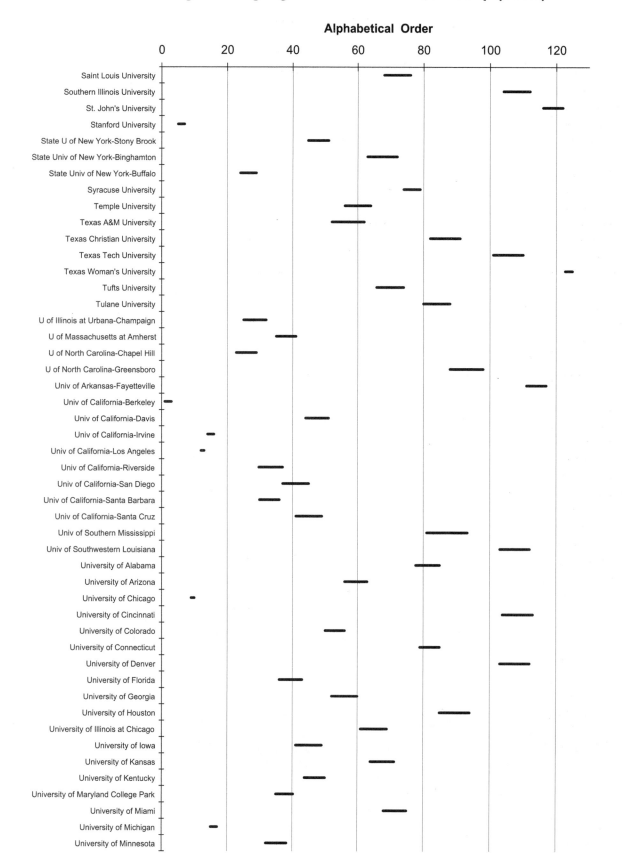

Chart 6-1B: Interquartile Range of Program Rankings* in English Language and Literature—Bootstrap (Cont.)

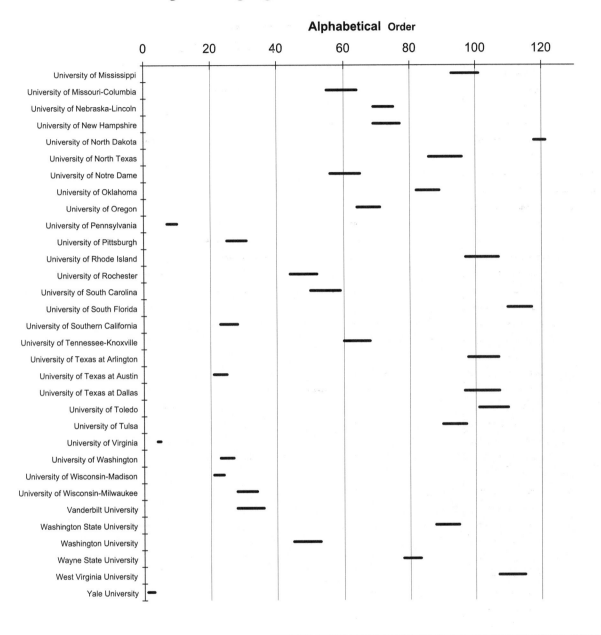

*Data from 1995 Study.

Chart 6-2A: Interquartile Range of Program Rankings* in Mathematics—Random Halves

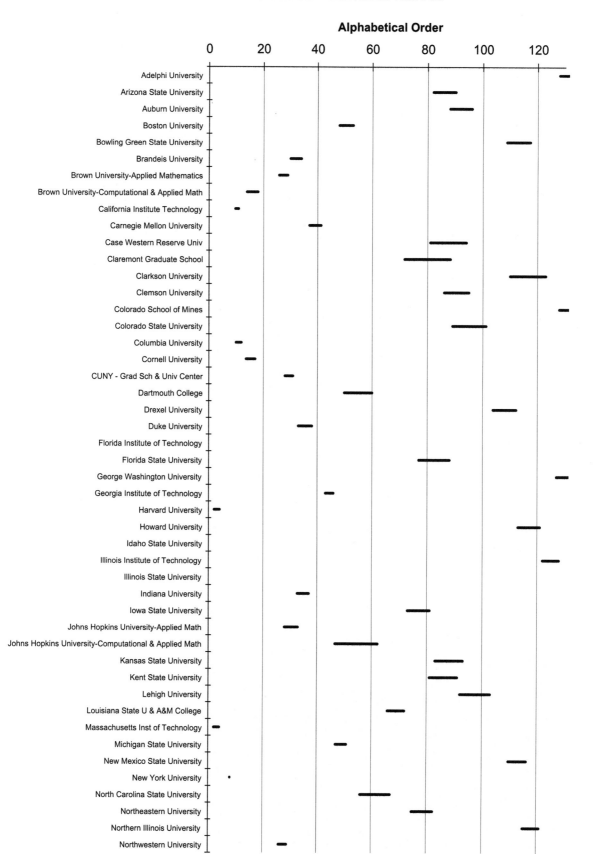

Chart 6-2A: Interquartile Range of Program Rankings* in Mathematics—Random Halves (Cont.)

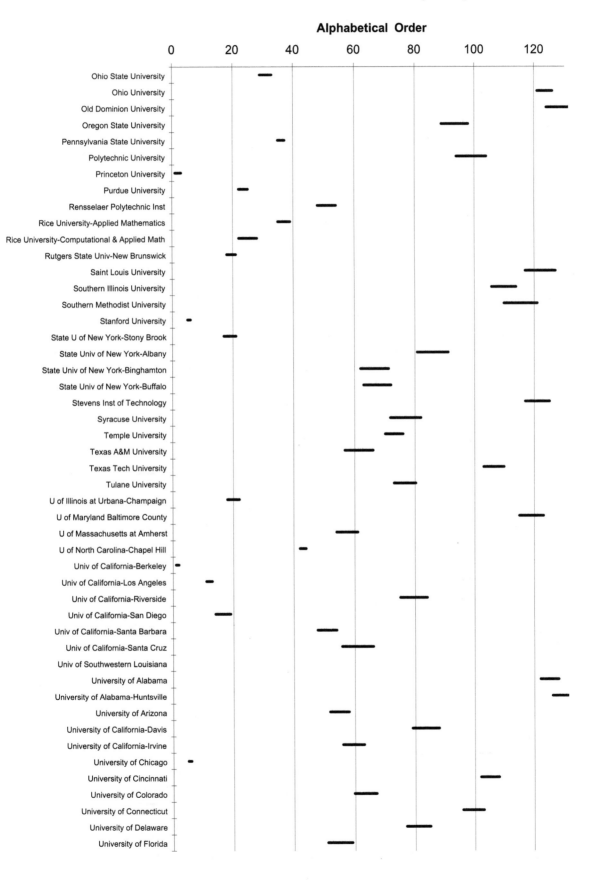

Chart 6-2A: Interquartile Range of Program Rankings* in Mathematics—Random Halves (Cont.)

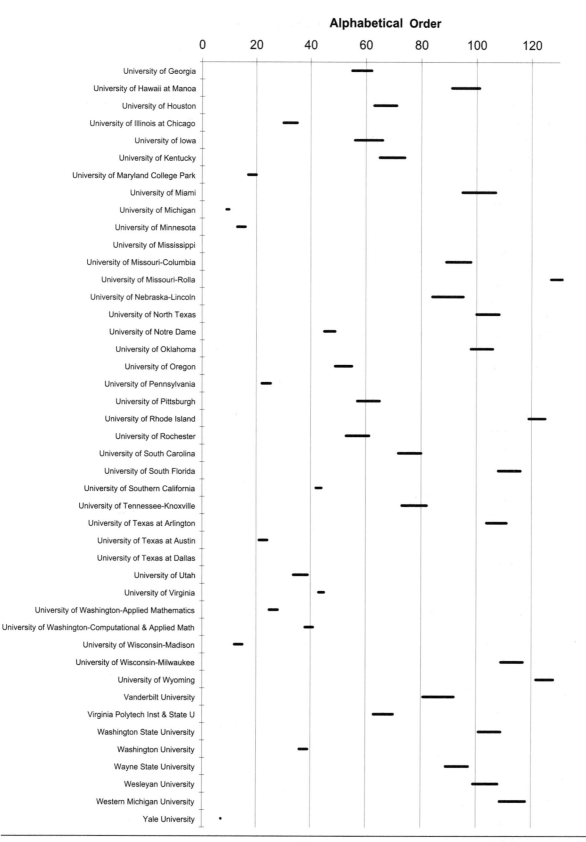

Chart 6-2B: Interquartile Range of Program Rankings* in Mathematics—Bootstrap

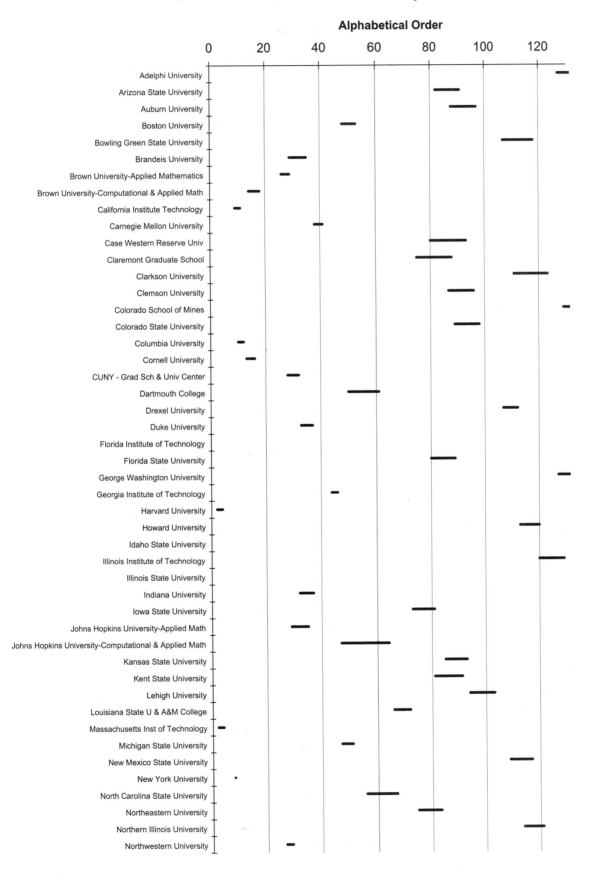

Chart 6-2B: Interquartile Range of Program Rankings* in Mathematics—Bootstrap (Cont.)

Chart 6-2B: Interquartile Range of Program Rankings* in Mathematics—Bootstrap (Cont.)

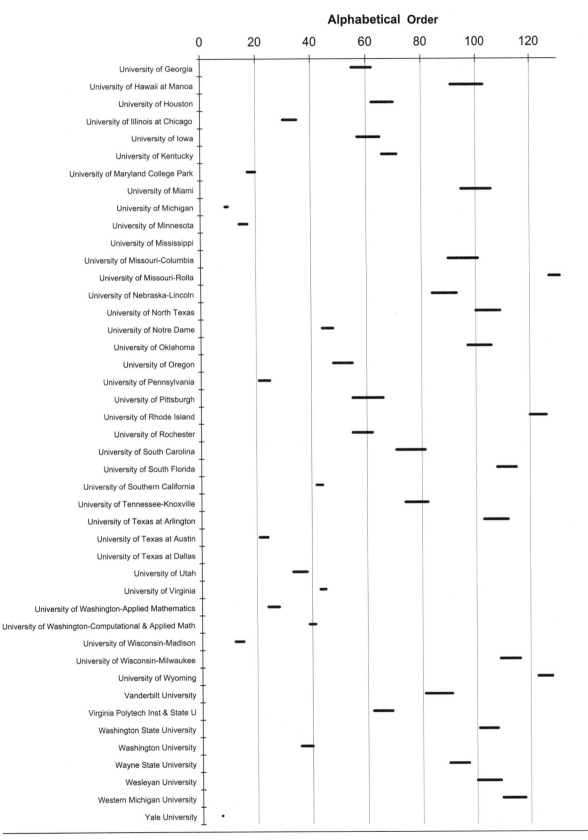

Alphabetical Order

*Data from 1995 Study.

TABLE 6-1A Interquartile Range of Program Rankings* in English Language and Literature - Random Halves

Institution	Rankings Quartiles 1st	3rd	Institution	Rankings Quartiles 1st	3rd
Arizona State University	75	82	U of North Carolina-Chapel Hill	23	29
Auburn University	85	93	U of North Carolina-Greensboro	89	98
Ball State University	110	117	Univ of Arkansas-Fayetteville	110	117
Baylor University	118	122	Univ of California-Berkeley	1	3
Boston College	59	68	Univ of California-Davis	45	50
Boston University	36	43	Univ of California-Irvine	14	16
Bowling Green State University	98	107	Univ of California-Los Angeles	12	13
Brandeis University	43	51	Univ of California-Riverside	30	38
Brown University	13	15	Univ of California-San Diego	36	43
Carnegie Mellon University	47	60	Univ of California-Santa Barbara	31	38
Case Western Reserve Univ	87	94	Univ of California-Santa Cruz	41	51
Catholic University of America	118	122	Univ of Southern Mississippi	83	92
Claremont Graduate School	76	89	Univ of Southwestern Louisiana	103	110
Columbia University	7	9	University of Alabama	76	83
Cornell University	6	8	University of Arizona	57	63
CUNY - Grad Sch & Univ Center	18	19	University of Chicago	8	10
Drew University	122	125	University of Cincinnati	103	111
Duke University	5	7	University of Colorado	49	58
Emory University	27	33	University of Connecticut	78	84
Florida State University	82	91	University of Denver	102	112
Fordham University	102	112	University of Florida	37	42
George Washington University	76	86	University of Georgia	53	60
Harvard University	1	2	University of Houston	86	93
Howard University	107	114	University of Illinois at Chicago	60	69
Idaho State University	124	126	University of Iowa	41	49
Illinois State University	100	109	University of Kansas	63	70
Indiana Univ of Pennsylvania	122	125	University of Kentucky	41	49
Indiana University	18	20	University of Maryland College Park	36	41
Johns Hopkins University	10	11	University of Miami	68	73
Kent State University	87	95	University of Michigan	15	17
Lehigh University	108	115	University of Minnesota	32	38
Louisiana State U & A&M College	55	64	University of Mississippi	94	102
Loyola University of Chicago	85	94	University of Missouri-Columbia	57	64
Miami University	72	78	University of Nebraska-Lincoln	69	75
Michigan State University	54	62	University of New Hampshire	70	77
Middle Tennessee State University	126	127	University of North Dakota	117	121
New York University	18	20	University of North Texas	86	94
Northern Illinois University	94	103	University of Notre Dame	56	65
Northwestern University	26	33	University of Oklahoma	81	87
Ohio State University	31	38	University of Oregon	64	69
Ohio University	99	110	University of Pennsylvania	7	10
Oklahoma State University	119	122	University of Pittsburgh	25	31
Pennsylvania State University	38	45	University of Rhode Island	98	107
Princeton University	13	14	University of Rochester	44	50
Purdue University	53	61	University of South Carolina	48	59
Rice University	49	60	University of South Florida	110	117
Rutgers State Univ-New Brunswick	15	17	University of Southern California	24	29
Saint Louis University	70	76	University of Tennessee-Knoxville	59	70
Southern Illinois University	104	113	University of Texas at Arlington	99	106
St. John's University	118	122	University of Texas at Austin	21	24
Stanford University	5	7	University of Texas at Dallas	98	105
State U of New York-Stony Brook	44	52	University of Toledo	101	110
State Univ of New York-Binghamton	63	71	University of Tulsa	90	98
State Univ of New York-Buffalo	25	29	University of Virginia	4	6
Syracuse University	74	79	University of Washington	22	26
Temple University	56	64	University of Wisconsin-Madison	21	24
Texas A&M University	53	62	University of Wisconsin-Milwaukee	27	36
Texas Christian University	84	97	Vanderbilt University	28	35
Texas Tech University	101	110	Washington State University	84	93
Texas Woman's University	122	125	Washington University	47	53
Tufts University	66	74	Wayne State University	77	84
Tulane University	81	89	West Virginia University	107	115
U of Illinois at Urbana-Champaign	25	31	Yale University	1	3
U of Massachusetts at Amherst	37	43			

*Data from 1995 Study.

TABLE 6-1B Interquartile Range of Program Rankings* in English Language and Literature - Bootstrap

Institution	Rankings Quartiles		Institution	Rankings Quartiles	
	1st	3rd		1st	3rd
Arizona State University	75	82	U of North Carolina-Chapel Hill	23	29
Auburn University	85	94	U of North Carolina-Greensboro	88	98
Ball State University	110	117	Univ of Arkansas-Fayetteville	111	117
Baylor University	119	122	Univ of California-Berkeley	1	3
Boston College	61	68	Univ of California-Davis	44	51
Boston University	36	45	Univ of California-Irvine	14	16
Bowling Green State University	97	106	Univ of California-Los Angeles	12	13
Brandeis University	43	51	Univ of California-Riverside	30	37
Brown University	13	15	Univ of California-San Diego	37	45
Carnegie Mellon University	46	57	Univ of California-Santa Barbara	30	36
Case Western Reserve Univ	88	96	Univ of California-Santa Cruz	41	49
Catholic University of America	118	122	Univ of Southern Mississippi	81	93
Claremont Graduate School	78	89	Univ of Southwestern Louisiana	103	112
Columbia University	6	9	University of Alabama	78	85
Cornell University	6	8	University of Arizona	56	63
CUNY - Grad Sch & Univ Center	17	19	University of Chicago	9	10
Drew University	122	125	University of Cincinnati	104	113
Duke University	5	7	University of Colorado	50	56
Emory University	29	34	University of Connecticut	79	85
Florida State University	83	91	University of Denver	103	112
Fordham University	105	113	University of Florida	36	43
George Washington University	77	84	University of Georgia	52	60
Harvard University	1	2	University of Houston	85	94
Howard University	103	114	University of Illinois at Chicago	61	69
Idaho State University	124	126	University of Iowa	41	49
Illinois State University	102	109	University of Kansas	64	71
Indiana Univ of Pennsylvania	123	125	University of Kentucky	44	50
Indiana University	18	20	University of Maryland College Park	35	40
Johns Hopkins University	10	11	University of Miami	68	75
Kent State University	88	96	University of Michigan	15	17
Lehigh University	109	116	University of Minnesota	32	38
Louisiana State U & A&M College	53	62	University of Mississippi	93	101
Loyola University of Chicago	85	96	University of Missouri-Columbia	55	64
Miami University	72	79	University of Nebraska-Lincoln	69	75
Michigan State University	55	64	University of New Hampshire	69	77
Middle Tennessee State University	126	127	University of North Dakota	118	121
New York University	18	20	University of North Texas	86	96
Northern Illinois University	94	101	University of Notre Dame	56	65
Northwestern University	27	33	University of Oklahoma	82	89
Ohio State University	30	39	University of Oregon	64	71
Ohio University	99	108	University of Pennsylvania	7	10
Oklahoma State University	118	122	University of Pittsburgh	25	31
Pennsylvania State University	39	45	University of Rhode Island	97	107
Princeton University	13	15	University of Rochester	44	52
Purdue University	54	63	University of South Carolina	50	59
Rice University	52	62	University of South Florida	110	117
Rutgers State Univ-New Brunswick	15	18	University of Southern California	23	28
Saint Louis University	68	76	University of Tennessee-Knoxville	60	68
Southern Illinois University	104	112	University of Texas at Arlington	98	107
St. John's University	116	122	University of Texas at Austin	21	25
Stanford University	5	7	University of Texas at Dallas	97	107
State U of New York-Stony Brook	45	51	University of Toledo	101	110
State Univ of New York-Binghamton	63	72	University of Tulsa	90	97
State Univ of New York-Buffalo	24	29	University of Virginia	4	5
Syracuse University	74	79	University of Washington	23	27
Temple University	56	64	University of Wisconsin-Madison	21	24
Texas A&M University	52	62	University of Wisconsin-Milwaukee	28	34
Texas Christian University	82	91	Vanderbilt University	28	36
Texas Tech University	101	110	Washington State University	88	95
Texas Woman's University	123	125	Washington University	45	53
Tufts University	66	74	Wayne State University	78	83
Tulane University	80	88	West Virginia University	107	115
U of Illinois at Urbana-Champaign	25	32	Yale University	1	3
U of Massachusetts at Amherst	35	41			

*Data from 1995 Study.

TABLE 6-2A Interquartile Range of Program Rankings* in Mathematics - Random Halves

Institution	Rankings Quartiles		Institution	Rankings Quartiles	
	1st	3rd		1st	3rd
Adelphi University	128	133	Rice University-Applied Mathematics	35	39
Arizona State University	82	90	Rice University-Computational & Applied Math	22	28
Auburn University	88	96	Rutgers State Univ-New Brunswick	18	21
Boston University	48	53	Saint Louis University	117	127
Bowling Green State University	109	117	Southern Illinois University	106	114
Brandeis University	30	34	Southern Methodist University	110	121
Brown University-Applied Mathematics	26	29	Stanford University	5	6
Brown University-Computational & Applied Math	14	18	State U of New York-Stony Brook	17	21
California Institute Technology	10	11	State Univ of New York-Albany	81	91
Carnegie Mellon University	37	41	State Univ of New York-Binghamton	62	71
Case Western Reserve Univ	81	94	State Univ of New York-Buffalo	63	72
Claremont Graduate School	72	88	Stevens Inst of Technology	117	125
Clarkson University	110	123	Syracuse University	72	82
Clemson University	86	95	Temple University	70	76
Colorado School of Mines	128	133	Texas A&M University	57	66
Colorado State University	89	101	Texas Tech University	103	110
Columbia University	10	12	Tulane University	73	80
Cornell University	14	17	U of Illinois at Urbana-Champaign	18	22
CUNY - Grad Sch & Univ Center	28	31	U of Maryland Baltimore County	115	123
Dartmouth College	50	60	U of Massachusetts at Amherst	54	61
Drexel University	104	112	U of North Carolina-Chapel Hill	42	44
Duke University	33	38	Univ of California-Berkeley	1	2
Florida Institute of Technology	132	135	Univ of California-Los Angeles	11	13
Florida State University	77	88	Univ of California-Riverside	75	84
George Washington University	127	133	Univ of California-San Diego	14	19
Georgia Institute of Technology	43	46	Univ of California-Santa Barbara	48	54
Harvard University	2	4	Univ of California-Santa Cruz	56	66
Howard University	113	121	Univ of Southwestern Louisiana	132	134
Idaho State University	137	138	University of Alabama	122	128
Illinois Institute of Technology	122	128	University of Alabama-Huntsville	126	132
Illinois State University	139	139	University of Arizona	52	58
Indiana University	33	37	University of California-Davis	79	88
Iowa State University	73	81	University of California-Irvine	56	63
Johns Hopkins University-Applied Math	28	33	University of Chicago	5	6
Johns Hopkins University-Computational & Applied Math	47	62	University of Cincinnati	102	108
Kansas State University	83	93	University of Colorado	60	67
Kent State University	81	91	University of Connecticut	96	103
Lehigh University	92	103	University of Delaware	77	85
Louisiana State U & A&M College	66	72	University of Florida	51	59
Massachusetts Inst of Technology	2	4	University of Georgia	55	62
Michigan State University	47	51	University of Hawaii at Manoa	91	101
New Mexico State University	110	116	University of Houston	63	71
New York University	8	8	University of Illinois at Chicago	30	35
North Carolina State University	56	67	University of Iowa	56	66
Northeastern University	75	82	University of Kentucky	65	74
Northern Illinois University	115	121	University of Maryland College Park	17	20
Northwestern University	26	29	University of Miami	95	107
Ohio State University	29	33	University of Michigan	9	10
Ohio University	121	126	University of Minnesota	13	16
Old Dominion University	124	132	University of Mississippi	135	136
Oregon State University	89	98	University of Missouri-Columbia	89	98
Pennsylvania State University	35	37	University of Missouri-Rolla	127	132
Polytechnic University	94	104	University of Nebraska-Lincoln	84	95
Princeton University	1	3	University of North Texas	100	108
Purdue University	22	25	University of Notre Dame	45	49
Rensselaer Polytechnic Inst	48	54	University of Oklahoma	98	106
			University of Oregon	49	55

Institution	Rankings Quartiles	
	1st	3rd
University of Pennsylvania	22	25
University of Pittsburgh	57	65
University of Rhode Island	119	125
University of Rochester	53	61
University of South Carolina	72	80
University of South Florida	108	116
University of Southern California	42	44
University of Tennessee-Knoxville	73	82
University of Texas at Arlington	104	111
University of Texas at Austin	21	24
University of Texas at Dallas	136	138
University of Utah	34	39
University of Virginia	43	45
University of Washington-Applied Mathematics	25	28
University of Washington-Computational & Applied Math	38	41
University of Wisconsin-Madison	12	15
University of Wisconsin-Milwaukee	109	117
University of Wyoming	122	128
Vanderbilt University	81	92
Virginia Polytech Inst & State U	63	70
Washington State University	101	109
Washington University	36	39
Wayne State University	89	97
Wesleyan University	99	108
Western Michigan University	109	118
Yale University	7	7

*Data from 1995 Study.

TABLE 6-2B Interquartile Range of Program Rankings* in Mathematics - Bootstrap

Institution	Rankings Quartiles 1st	3rd
Adelphi University	127	133
Arizona State University	82	91
Auburn University	88	97
Boston University	48	53
Bowling Green State University	107	118
Brandeis University	29	35
Brown University-Applied Mathematics	26	29
Brown University-Computational & Applied Math	14	18
California Institute Technology	9	11
Carnegie Mellon University	38	41
Case Western Reserve Univ	80	93
Claremont Graduate School	75	88
Clarkson University	111	123
Clemson University	87	96
Colorado School of Mines	129	134
Colorado State University	89	98
Columbia University	10	12
Cornell University	13	16
CUNY - Grad Sch & Univ Center	28	32
Dartmouth College	50	61
Drexel University	107	112
Duke University	33	37
Florida Institute of Technology	133	135
Florida State University	80	89
George Washington University	127	133
Georgia Institute of Technology	44	46
Harvard University	2	4
Howard University	113	120
Idaho State University	137	138
Illinois Institute of Technology	120	129
Illinois State University	139	139
Indiana University	32	37
Iowa State University	73	81
Johns Hopkins University-Applied Math	29	35
Johns Hopkins University-Computational & Applied Math	47	64
Kansas State University	85	93
Kent State University	81	91
Lehigh University	94	103
Louisiana State U & A&M College	66	72
Massachusetts Inst of Technology	2	4
Michigan State University	47	51
New Mexico State University	109	117
New York University	8	8
North Carolina State University	56	67
Northeastern University	75	83
Northern Illinois University	114	121
Northwestern University	27	29
Ohio State University	28	33
Ohio University	120	125
Old Dominion University	125	131
Oregon State University	87	96
Pennsylvania State University	35	38
Polytechnic University	94	103
Princeton University	1	3
Purdue University	23	26
Rensselaer Polytechnic Inst	48	55

Institution	Rankings Quartiles 1st	3rd
Rice University-Applied Mathematics	34	39
Rice University-Computational & Applied Math	23	29
Rutgers State Univ-New Brunswick	17	20
Saint Louis University	118	127
Southern Illinois University	106	115
Southern Methodist University	113	123
Stanford University	5	6
State U of New York-Stony Brook	18	22
State Univ of New York-Albany	81	91
State Univ of New York-Binghamton	62	74
State Univ of New York-Buffalo	64	72
Stevens Inst of Technology	116	126
Syracuse University	73	81
Temple University	71	76
Texas A&M University	57	65
Texas Tech University	102	111
Tulane University	72	79
U of Illinois at Urbana-Champaign	19	22
U of Maryland Baltimore County	117	124
U of Massachusetts at Amherst	54	60
U of North Carolina-Chapel Hill	42	44
Univ of California-Berkeley	1	2
Univ of California-Los Angeles	11	13
Univ of California-Riverside	74	83
Univ of California-San Diego	15	18
Univ of California-Santa Barbara	48	54
Univ of California-Santa Cruz	56	66
Univ of Southwestern Louisiana	132	135
University of Alabama	122	128
University of Alabama-Huntsville	128	132
University of Arizona	50	57
University of California-Davis	80	88
University of California-Irvine	56	64
University of Chicago	5	6
University of Cincinnati	101	108
University of Colorado	60	66
University of Connecticut	97	102
University of Delaware	77	84
University of Florida	53	60
University of Georgia	55	62
University of Hawaii at Manoa	91	103
University of Houston	62	70
University of Illinois at Chicago	30	35
University of Iowa	57	65
University of Kentucky	66	71
University of Maryland College Park	17	20
University of Miami	95	106
University of Michigan	9	10
University of Minnesota	14	17
University of Mississippi	135	136
University of Missouri-Columbia	90	101
University of Missouri-Rolla	127	131
University of Nebraska-Lincoln	84	93
University of North Texas	100	109
University of Notre Dame	44	48
University of Oklahoma	97	106
University of Oregon	48	55

Institution	Rankings Quartiles	
	1st	3rd
University of Pennsylvania	21	25
University of Pittsburgh	55	66
University of Rhode Island	120	126
University of Rochester	55	62
University of South Carolina	71	81
University of South Florida	108	115
University of Southern California	42	44
University of Tennessee-Knoxville	74	82
University of Texas at Arlington	103	112
University of Texas at Austin	21	24
University of Texas at Dallas	137	138
University of Utah	33	38
University of Virginia	43	45
University of Washington-Applied Mathematics	24	28
University of Washington-Computational & Applied Math	39	41
University of Wisconsin-Madison	12	15
University of Wisconsin-Milwaukee	109	116
University of Wyoming	123	128
Vanderbilt University	81	91
Virginia Polytech Inst & State U	62	69
Washington State University	101	108
Washington University	36	40
Wayne State University	90	97
Wesleyan University	100	109
Western Michigan University	110	118
Yale University	7	7

*Data from 1995 Study.

7

General Conclusions and Recommendations

The Committee to Examine the Methodology to Assess Research-Doctorate Programs was presented with the task of examining the methodologies used in the 1995 National Research Council Study, *Research-Doctorate Programs in the United States: Continuity and Change* (referred to throughout this report as the "1995 Study") to determine the feasibility of significant improvements. The previous chapters have made specific recommendations on how to conduct an assessment of research-doctorate programs under the assumption that it will be done. The more fundamental question remains to be addressed: Should another study be carried out at all? This chapter presents the Committee's conclusions on this and other general issues along with the reasons for supporting them.

SHOULD ANOTHER ASSESSMENT OF RESEARCH-DOCTORATE PROGRAMS BE UNDERTAKEN BY THE NATIONAL RESEARCH COUNCIL?

The Committee was asked to examine the methodology of the 1995 Study and to identify both its strengths and its weaknesses. Where weaknesses were found, it was asked to suggest methods to remedy them.

The strengths of the 1995 Study identified by the Committee were:

• *Wide acceptance.* It was widely accepted, quoted, and utilized as an authoritative source of information on the quality of doctoral programs.
• *Comprehensiveness.* It covered 41 of the largest fields of doctoral study.
• *Transparency.* Its methodology was clearly stated.
• *Temporal continuity.* For most programs, it maintained continuity with the NRC study carried out 10 years earlier.

Finally, it should be noted that the study was a useful tool for doctoral programs to improve themselves and hence to improve doctoral education. A frequent use of the study by administrators is to examine the characteristics of programs that are rated more highly than their own. If the study is carried out again, it would provide the quantitative basis for such analyses.

The weaknesses were:

• *Data presentation.* The emphasis on exact numerical rankings encouraged users of the study to draw spurious inferences of precision.
• *Flawed measurement of educational quality.* The reputational measure of program effectiveness in graduate education, derived from a question asked of faculty raters, confounded research reputation and educational quality.
• *Emphasis on the reputational measure of scholarly quality.* This emphasis gave users the impression that a "soft" criterion, subject to "halo" and "size effects," was being relied on for the assessment of programs.
• *Obsolescence of data.* The period of 10 years between studies was viewed as too long.
• *Poor dissemination of results.* The presentation of the study data was in a form that was difficult for potential students to use since it was inaccessible and difficult to interpret.
• *Use of an outdated or inappropriate taxonomy of fields.* Particularly for the biological sciences, the taxonomy did not reflect the current organization of graduate programs in many institutions.
• *Inadequate validation of data.* Data were not sent back to providers for a check on accuracy, and some unnecessary errors were propagated.

The weaknesses listed above were addressed in earlier chapters, but in addition to these difficulties, it must be noted that assessments of research-doctorate programs are costly in the direct costs of staff and committee time, but far greater and invisible costs are incurred by university faculty and administrative personnel in amassing data for inclusion in the study. The benefits of the NRC study must outweigh these costs if it is to be undertaken.

One other issue to be addressed is the possibility of duplicative studies. Broad rankings of doctoral programs in some fields are conducted periodically by *US News and World Report* (USN&WR). Unless the NRC study differs in important respects from that study, there seems little reason to incur the known costs.

Both the USN&WR and the NRC reports publish reputational rankings, but the resemblance ends there. USN&WR rankings appear with somewhat greater frequency, and they cover a more limited set of fields outside of professional schools. With the exception of engineering, USN&WR publishes only reputational rankings (as of their 2004 edition). Quantitative data are collected for engineering, but USN&WR employs a weighted average of quantitative data and reputational ratings to arrive at a composite ranking. The problem with this approach is that any ranking based on weighted averages of quantitative indicators is necessarily subjective. They represent an implementation of someone's prejudices regarding the relative importance of the various indicators.

There are additional technical objections to the USN&WR rankings. For those fields for which there is overlap with the NRC fields, the response rates for USN&WR were 10-20 percentage points below those obtained for the 1995 NRC report. Even more importantly, USN&WR targets administrators as respondents and asks their views of programs in fields outside their area of expertise. The NRC makes every effort to obtain ratings from within-field peers who are primarily faculty.

The differences between the two studies also reflect a difference in audience. USN&WR is aimed directly at the potential student and purports to contain material that would be helpful to students applying to graduate school. The 1995 NRC Study was primarily directed to faculty, administrators, and scholars of higher education. It was not especially user-friendly. In fact, Brendan Maher, a co-author of the 1995 Study, subsequently wrote a guide for students and others.[1]

Because of the transparent way in which NRC studies present their data, the more extensive coverage of fields outside of professional schools, their focus on peer ratings, and the relatively high response rates they obtain, there is clearly value added in having the NRC conduct the assessment once again. However, two questions still remain: Do reputational ratings do more harm than good to the enterprise that they seek to assess? And, does the fact that ratings are published by a prestigious organization, such as the NRC, lend more credence to rankings than should be due?

Ratings would be harmful if they gave a distorted view of the graduate enterprise or if they encouraged behavior inimical to improving its quality. The Committee believes that a number of steps recommended in previous chapters would minimize these risks. Presenting ratings as ranges would diminish the focus of some administrators on hiring decisions designed purely to "move up in the rankings." Ascertaining whether programs track student outcomes would encourage programs to pay more attention to improving student outcomes. Asking students about the education they have received would encourage programs to focus on graduate education as well as on research. Expanding the set of quantitative measures would permit deeper investigations into components of a program that contribute to a reputation for quality. More frequent updating of these data would provide more timely and objective assessments. A careful analysis of the correlates of reputation would improve public understanding of the factors that contribute to a highly reputed graduate program.

Recommendation 1: The assessment of both the scholarly quality of doctoral programs and the educational practices of these programs is important to higher education, its funders, its students, and to society. The National Research Council should continue to conduct such assessments on a regular basis.

One of the major objections to previous NRC studies is that they are performed only every 10 years. The reason for this is a practical one. A national survey of graduate faculty is an enormous undertaking and changes in scholarly quality occur slowly. Little new information would be gained at a high cost if faculty were to be questioned frequently about a slowly changing phenomenon. The ability to gather quantitative data electronically at little cost, however, makes possible more frequent reporting of quantitative data. We will attempt to produce periodically and, ideally, annually updatable proxy assessments based on quantitative information. The Committee believes that Web-based data gathering should be a part of the next study and suggests the establishment of an updateable database on graduate programs. Further, once a statistical analysis of the relationship between quantitative measures and the reputational measure has been conducted for each field, it will be possible to construct a "synthetic reputational measure," constructed under the assumption that the parameters that relate the quantitative measures to reputation have held steady over time, but that the values themselves have changed. Although the measure is weighted, the weights are not subjective except in the sense they will be statistically determined and the combination of measures that provide the best fit will be used to construct the indicator for subsequent years. The measures and their parameters are then frozen in time, although the values of the measures may change.

---

[1]"How to Read the 1995 National Research Council Report *Research-Doctorate Programs in the United States.*" 1996.

Recommendation 2: Although scholarly reputation and the composition of program faculty change slowly and can be assessed over a decade, quantitative indicators that are related to quality may change more rapidly and should be updated on a regular and more frequent basis than scholarly reputation. The Committee recommends investigation of the construction of a synthetic measure of reputation for each field, based on statistically derived combinations of quantitative measures. This synthetic measure could be recalculated periodically and, if possible, annually.

As described in Chapter 6, reputational rankings depend on the dispersion of the aggregated ratings of many raters. This dispersion is relatively narrow for the very best programs but increases for other programs simply because information about such programs is not as widely known. A number of factors may contribute to this phenomenon—lack of rater knowledge about the program, the likelihood that smaller programs may specialize in some subfields but not others, and the fact that different raters value different dimensions of program quality when they assign ratings.

Although it may greatly disappoint those programs which would like to boast about their place in the ratings, the Committee believes that presenting ratings in a way that portrays dispersion (or lack of rater agreement about the exact ranking) would improve the usefulness of the ratings.

Recommendation 3: The presentation of reputational ratings should be modified so as to minimize the drawing of a spurious inference of precision in program ranking.

In addition to the quantitative measures collected in the 1995 Study, additional measures would add to the ability of study users to analyze the correlates of reputation. These are discussed in detail in Chapter 4, but include data on electronic acquisitions by libraries and field-specific measures, such as laboratory space in the sciences, and number of books in the humanities.

Recommendation 4: Data for quantitative measures should be collected regularly and made accessible in a Web-readable format. These measures should be reported whenever significantly updated data are available. (See Recommendation 4.1 for details.)

The education of doctoral students for a wide range of employment beyond that in academia has become an object of growing attention in the educational policy community and among the students themselves. In addition to collecting data on educational practices and resources, the Committee proposes that the next NRC study collect data from advanced-to-candidacy students in a small number of fields in order to assesses their educational experiences, their research productivity, program practices, and institutional and program environments. Further, although the Committee realizes that it would not be feasible to conduct a large study of outcomes, it believes that information on whether programs collect and publish such information would be valuable to potential students.

Recommendation 5: Comparable information on educational processes should be collected directly from advanced-to-candidacy students in selected programs and reported. Whether or not individual programs monitor outcomes for their graduates should be reported.

The Committee constructed a taxonomy of fields for the proposed study that reflected changes that have taken place in the past decade, especially in the biological sciences. Although it was not able to identify many interdisciplinary fields that offered doctoral programs, it did recommend a new category that would present data on such fields as they emerged. Many such fields may still be included in more traditional programs. The committee appointed to conduct the proposed study should consider the exact details of the taxonomy. This is an open question, still subject to review.

Recommendation 6: The taxonomy of fields should be changed from that used in the 1995 Study to incorporate additional fields with large Ph.D. production. The agricultural sciences should be added to the taxonomy and efforts should be made to include basic biomedical fields in medical schools. A new category, "emerging fields," should be included.

In the 1995 Study, data were not send back to the providers for validation. This introduced a number of errors. For example, for multicampus institution whole programs were omitted and a number of faculty lists were inaccurate. The next study should make sure this does not happen. This is made much more feasible by the availability of information technology.

Recommendation 7: All data that are collected should be validated by the providers.

There is an increasing trans-border flow of doctoral students between Canadian and U.S. doctoral programs. Although there are differences between the national systems, there are many similarities as well. The Committee believes that the inclusion of Canadian research-doctorate programs would be useful to programs in both countries.

Recommendation 8: If the recommendation of the Canadian Research-Doctorate Quality Assessment Study, which is currently underway, is to participate in the proposed NRC study, Canadian doctoral programs should be included in the next NRC assessment.

The past decade has seen enormous strides in information technology. It is now feasible, as demonstrated by the pilot trials, to collect data using Web questionnaires. This is a cost-effective technology, saving not only postage but also the time of coders and permitting rapid validation of data. Electronic technology can and should also play an important role in the dissemination of the report. Databases can be made available on-line, as can simple analytic software that would enable users to select peer institutions as well as conduct comparative analyses, while maintaining rater confidentiality. The database for the proposed study should be designed with this sort of dissemination in mind.

Recommendation 9: Extensive use of electronic Web-based means of dissemination should be utilized for both the initial report and periodic updates (cf. Recommendations 2 and 4).

THE FORM OF THE PROPOSED STUDY

The 1995 Study was disseminated as a book of 740 pages, 64 pages of which comprised the text. The remaining pages contained tables of data and rankings. The bulky study was also made available on the Web. Two years later, a CD was published with these data and supplemental data on the ratings of raters. Electronic technology now makes it possible to immediately publish all the data, aggregated to preserve rater confidentiality, on the Web. The same technology makes it possible for data from the next study to be pre-released to designated researchers for analytic studies and for those studies to be published as the print "report" of the study. Furthermore, a Web-based release makes it possible to provide analytical tools to users so that they can compose and rate programs using *à la carte* quantitative weights of their own choosing. The Committee believes strongly that publication of the data alone, without an exploration of its strengths and limitations, should not happen again. The funding of analytic work should be built into the study and appear as a prominent part of the report.

Finally, since the report will have considerably more information of interest to students, it would be very helpful to include as an integral part of the report a section, entitled *How to Read This Report,* similar to the guide written by Brendan Maher in 1996.

References

Association of American Universities Committee on Graduate Education. 1998. Report and Recommendations. Washington, D.C.

Bowen, W. G., and N. L. Rudenstine. 1992. In Pursuit of the PhD. Princeton, N.J.: Princeton University Press.

Cartter, A. M. 1966. An Assessment of Quality in Graduate Education. Washington, D.C.: American Council on Education.

Cole, J., and S. Cole. 1973. Social Stratification in Science. Chicago, Ill.: The University of Chicago Press.

Committee on Science, Engineering, and Public Policy (COSEPUP). 1995. Reshaping the Graduate Education of Scientists and Engineers, Executive Summary. Washington, D.C.: The National Academy Press.

Duderstadt, J. J. 2000. A University for the 21st Century. Ann Arbor, Mich.: The University of Michigan Press.

Ehrenberg, R. G., and P. J. Hurst. 1998. The 1995 Ratings of Doctoral Programs: A Hedonic Model. The Economics of Education Review. 17(2):137-148.

Ehrenberg, R. G., and P. J. Hurst. 1996. The 1995 Ratings of Doctoral Programs: A Hedonic Model. Change. May/June:46-50.

Gaff, J. G., A. S. Pruitt-Logan, and R. Weibl. 2000. Building the Faculty We Need. Washington, D.C.: Association of American Colleges and Universities.

Goldberger, M. L., B. A. Maher, and P. E. Flattau. 1995. Research-Doctorate Programs in the United States: Continuity and Change. Washington, D.C.: National Academy Press.

Golde, C. M. July 2001 draft. Overview of Doctoral Education Initiatives, Studies and Reports: 1990-Present. Carnegie Foundation for the Advancement of Teaching Report.

Golde, C. M., and T. M. Dore. 2001. At Cross Purposes: What the experiences of today's doctoral students reveal about doctoral education. Report prepared for The Pew Charitable Trusts. Philadlephia, Pa.

Graham, H. D., and N. Diamond. 1997. The Rise of American Research Universities. Baltimore, Md.: Johns Hopkins University Press.

Graham, H. D., and N. Diamond. 1999. Academic Departments and the Ratings Game. Chronicle of Higher Education June 18:B6.

Jones, L. V., G. Lindzey, and P. E. Coggeshall. 1982. An Assessment of Research-Doctorate Programs in the United States. Washington, D.C.: National Academy Press.

Junn, J., and R. Brooks. 2000. A Brief Analysis of the 1992-93 Reputational Data in the 1995 NRC Report. Report submitted to the NRC, September 14.

LaPidus, J. 2000. Great Expectations: The Role of the American University in the 21st Century in J. Hamblin, ed., A Walk Through Graduate Education: Selected Papers and Speeches of Jules B. LaPidus. Washington, D.C.: Council of Graduate Schools.

Lorden, J., and L. Martin. n.d. Toward a Better Way to Rate Research Doctoral Programs. A position paper prepared for the NASULGC's Council on Research Policy and Graduate Education. See *http://www.nasulgc.org/publications/towards_a_better_way.pdf*.

Maher, B. A. 1996. How to Read the 1995 National Research Council Report Research-Doctorate Programs in the United States: A Guide for Students and Others. Washington, D.C.: National Academy Press.

The National Association of Graduate and Professional Students. 2000. *2000 NAGPS Survey. http://www.nagps.org*.

National Science Foundation. 2001. Employment Preferences and Outcomes of Recent Science and Engineering Doctorate Holders in the Labor Market. NSF-02-304. October 30. Arlington, Va.

National Science Foundation. 2002. Science and Engineering Doctorate Awards: 2001. NSF-03-300. Ch. 3:2-3. Arlington, Va.

Nerad, M., and J. Cerny. 1999. Postdoctoral Patterns, Career Advancement, and Problems. Science 285(3 September):1533-35.

Nerad, M., and J. Cerny. 1999. From Rumors to Facts: Career Outcomes of English Ph.D.s—Results from the Ph.Ds—Ten Years later Study. Council of Graduate Schools Communicator 32(7, Special Fall Issue): 1-11. Reprinted in Association of Departments of English Bulletin, winter 2000:124.

Nerad, M., and J. Cerny. 2002. Postdoctoral Appointments and Employment Patterns of Science and Engineering Doctoral Recipients Ten-plus Years after Ph.D. Completion: Selected Results from the Ph.Ds – Ten Years Later Study. Council of Graduate Schools Communicator September issue.

Maresi Nerad, Rebecca Aanerud, and Joseph Cerny, "So You Want to Be a Professor!: Lessons from the 'PhDs-Ten Years Later' Study" Ph.D.s-Ten Years Later: Implication for the Preparation of Future Faculty," in Donald Wulff and Ann Austin. Enriching Graduate Education to Prepare the Next Generation of Faculty: Challenges, Research and Practice, Jossey Bass (forth coming)

Nyquist, J. D., and B. J. Woodford. 2000. Re-envisioning the Ph.D.: What Concerns Do We Have? Booklet produced for Re-envisioning the Ph.D. Conference, April 13-15, 2000. Seattle, Wash.: Center for Instructional Development and Research and the University of Washington.

Nyquist, J. D., L. Manning, D. H. Wulff, A. E. Austin, J. Sprague, P. Fraser, C. Calcagno, and B. Woodford. 1999. On the Road to Becoming a Professor : The Graduate Student Experience. Change 31(3):18-27.

Peterson. 1999. Peterson's Graduate and Professional Programs: An Overview, 33rd edition. Princeton, N.J.

Roose, K. D., and C. J. Andersen. 1970. A Rating of Graduate Programs. Washington, D.C.: American Council on Education.

Webster, D.S., and T. Skinner. 1996. Rating Ph.D. Programs: What the
    NRC Report Says ... and Doesn't Say. Change May/June: 23-44.
Zuckerman, H., and J. S. Meisel. 2000. The Foundation's Programs for
    Research Universities and Humanistic Scholarship in the Andrew W.
    Mellon Foundation 2000 Annual Report (*www.mellon.org/Annual*).

Appendixes

Appendix A

Committee and Panel Member Biographical Sketches

1. Committee to Examine the Methodology for the Assessment of Research-Doctorate Programs
2. Panel on Taxonomy and Interdisciplinarity
3. Panel on Quantitative Measures
4. Panel on Reputational Measures and Data Presentation
5. Panel on Student Processes and Outcomes

COMMITTEE TO EXAMINE THE METHODOLOGY FOR THE ASSESSMENT OF RESEARCH-DOCTORATE PROGRAMS

Biographical Sketches

JEREMIAH P. OSTRIKER, Ph.D. (NAS), Committee Chair, is a professor of astrophysical sciences at Princeton University and Plumian Professor of Astronomy and Experimental Philosophy at the University of Cambridge. He received his B.A. in physics and chemistry from Harvard University and his Ph.D. in astrophysics from the University of Chicago. After a postdoctoral fellowship at Cambridge University, Dr. Ostriker served on the faculty at Princeton University as a professor (1966-present), as department chair and director of the Princeton University Observatory (1979-1995), and as university provost (1995-2001). During his tenure as provost, Princeton received a major grant from the Mellon Foundation to improve doctoral education in the humanities. He has received many awards and honors, including membership in the National Academy of Sciences (NAS) and in 2001, the U.S. National Medal of Science. He has served on several National Research Council (NRC) and National Academies committees, including the NAS Council and the NRC Governing Board. Dr. Ostriker also served as a member of the Panel on Quantitative Measures.

ELTON D. ABERLE, Ph.D., is Dean of the College of Agricultural and Life Sciences at the University of Wisconsin-Madison. He received his B.S. from Kansas State University in 1962, his M.S. from Michigan State University in 1965, and his Ph.D. from Michigan State University in food sciences in 1967. Previously, Dr. Aberle held administrative positions at the University of Nebraska-Lincoln's Institute of Agriculture and Natural Resources, and a faculty position at Purdue University. His research and teaching background is in muscle biology, and animal and food sciences. Dr. Aberle has received teaching and research awards from the American Society of Animal Sciences and the American Meat Science Association, and is a Fellow of the American Association for the Advancement of Science and the American Society of Animal Science. He also served on the Panel on Taxonomy and Interdisciplinarity.

JOHN BRAUMAN, Ph.D. (NAS), is the J.G. Jackson-C.J. Jackson Professor of Chemistry and Cognizant Dean for the Natural Sciences at Stanford University. He received his B.S. in 1959 from the Massachusetts Institute of Technology and his Ph.D. in 1963 from the University of California-Berkeley. Dr. Brauman's research is directed toward understanding how molecules react and the factors that determine the rates and products of chemical reactions. The principal areas of his research involve the spectroscopy, photochemistry, reaction dynamics, and reaction mechanisms of ions in the gas phase. Dr. Brauman is a member of the National Academy of Sciences (NAS), a Fellow of the American Academy of Arts and Sciences as well as of the American Association for the Advancement of Science, and an Honorary Fellow of the California Academy of Sciences. He has received numerous honors, including an NAS Award in the Chemical Sciences and an American Chemical Society award in Pure Chemistry. In his role as Cognizant Dean he oversees the departments of: applied physics, biological sciences, history, mathematics, physics, psychology, statistics, and the Hopkins Marine Station. He also served on the Panel on Reputational Measures and Data Presentation.

GEORGE BUGLIARELLO, Sc.D. (NAE), is President Emeritus and University Professor at Polytechnic University, where he served as President (1973-94) and Chancellor (1994-2003). He holds a Dott. Ing. in 1951 from the University of Padua, an M.S. in 1954 from the University of Minnesota, and a Sc.D. in 1959 from Massachusetts Institute of Technology. Dr. Bugliarello has a range of administrative experience as professor and dean of engineering at the University of Illinois at Chicago Circle and as professor and chairman of the Biotechnology Program at Carnegie Mellon University. His honors and awards include: Member of the National Academy of Engineering (NAE), Founding Fellow of the American Institute for Medical and Biological Engineering, Fellow of the American Society for Engineering Education, Fellow of the American Society of Civil Engineers, and Fellow of the New York Academy of Sciences. Dr. Bugliarello is Past President of Sigma Xi—the Scientific Research Society, and was elected in 2003 to a four-year term as Foreign Secretary of the NAE. His research interests include biomedical engineering, fluid mechanics, computer languages, and socio-technology. He also served on the Panel on Taxonomy and Interdisciplinarity.

WALTER COHEN, Ph.D., currently serves as Vice Provost and Professor of Comparative Literature at Cornell University. He also served as Dean of the Graduate School. He did his undergraduate work at Stanford University. Dr. Cohen joined the Cornell faculty after receiving his doctorate from the University of California-Berkeley in 1980. His academic specialties are Renaissance drama, literary theory, and the history of European literature. From 1998-1999, he served as president of the Association of Graduate Schools. He also served as co-chair of the Panel on Taxonomy and Interdisciplinarity.

JONATHAN COLE, Ph.D., is the John Mitchell Mason Professor of the University and Provost at Columbia University. He joined the faculty at Columbia in 1968 and served as the Director of the Center for Social Sciences from 1979 to 1987, Vice Provost for Arts and Sciences from 1987 to 1989, and the Quetelet Professor of Social Sciences from 1989 to 2001. Dr. Cole's awards and honors include a Guggenheim Fellowship, Fellow of the Center for Advanced Study in the Behavioral Sciences, and Fellow of the American Academy of Arts and Sciences. He has published extensively on the growth of scientific knowledge, the social organization of peer review in science, and women in the scientific community. Dr. Cole was a member of the previous committee for the study of research-doctorate programs. He also served as co-chair of the Panel on Reputational Measures and Data Presentation.

RONALD GRAHAM, Ph.D. (NAS), is Irwin and Joan Jacobs Professor in the Department of Computer Science and Engineering at the University of California-San Diego and Chief Scientist at the California Institute for Telecommunication and Information Technology of the University of California-San Diego. He holds an M.A. and a Ph.D. in mathematics from the University of California-Berkeley as well as a B.S. in physics from the University of Alaska at Fairbanks. Dr. Graham served as Director of Information Sciences at AT&T Bell Laboratories for more than 30 years. He has held numerous professorships in mathematics and computer science at institutions such as Rutgers University, Princeton University, Stanford University, and the California Institute of Technology. Dr. Graham's research work focuses on various areas in combinatorics, number theory, graph theory, computational geometry and theoretical computer science and the analysis of algorithms. He has served on numerous NAS boards and committees. He is a member of the National Academy of Sciences and serves as NAS Treasurer. He is a Past President of the American Mathematical Society and currently serves as President of the Mathematical Association of America. He also served on the Panel on Quantitative Measures.

PAUL HOLLAND, Ph.D., holds the Frederic M. Lord Chair in Measurement and Statistics and is acting director of the Center for Statistical Theory and Practice at the Educational Testing Service (ETS). He earned a B.A. in mathematics from the University of Michigan, and an M.A. and a Ph.D. in statistics from Stanford University. Dr. Holland's association with ETS began in 1975 as Director of the Research Statistics Group. In 1986, he was appointed ETS's first Distinguished Research Scientist. In 1993, Dr. Holland joined the faculty at University of California-Berkeley as a professor in the Graduate School of Education and the Department of Statistics but returned in 2000 to his current position at ETS. His research interests include psychometrics, causal inference of educational interventions in non-experimental studies; multivariate analysis and the explanation of score scales. He also served as co-chair of the Panel on Reputational Measures and Data Presentation.

EARL LEWIS, Ph.D., is Dean of the Graduate School, Vice Provost for Academic Affairs-Graduate Studies, and the Elsa Barkley Brown and Robin D.G. Kelley Collegiate Professor of History and African-American Studies at the University of Michigan. He earned his undergraduate degree from Concordia College in Moorhead, Minnesota, where he majored in history and psychology, and earned his doctorate in history at the University of Minnesota. Dr. Lewis's first academic appointment was at the University of California-Berkeley, where he taught from 1984-89. He is past Chair of the Board of the Council of Graduate Schools, a member of the GRE Board, and National Chair of the Responsive Ph.D. project. Dr. Lewis is the author or editor of five books, including *In Their Own Interests: Race, Class and Power in Twentieth-Century Norfolk*. His awards include the Gustavus Myers Outstanding Book Award for the co-edited volume, *To Make Our World Anew,* and the *Chicago Tribune's* favorite book for 2001 recognition for *Love on Trial*. He also served on the Panel on Student Processes and Outcomes.

JOAN F. LORDEN, Ph.D., is Provost and Vice Chancellor for Academic Affairs at the University of North Carolina at Charlotte. She received a B.A. from the City College of New York and a Ph.D. from Yale University. Dr. Lorden served for over eight years as Dean of the Graduate School and Associate Provost for Research at the University of Alabama at Birmingham (UAB). During 2002-03, she was the Council of Graduate Schools (CGS) Dean-in-Residence at the Division of Graduate Education at the National Science Foundation and chaired the CGS Board of Directors. Dr. Lorden's research focuses on brain-behavior relationships. At UAB she organized the doctoral program in behavioral neuroscience and was a founding member and director of the university-wide interdisciplinary Graduate Training Program in Neuroscience. As Graduate Dean, Dr. Lorden fostered programs that increased opportunities for breadth of training among graduate students and served as the program director for an interdisciplinary biological sciences training grant. Throughout her tenure as graduate dean, she was actively involved in programs designed to improve the recruitment of women and minorities into doctoral programs in science and engineering, and received several grants to advance these goals. She also served as chair of the Panel on Student Processes and Outcomes.

LOUIS MAHEU, Ph.D., is Dean and Vice President of Graduate Studies of the Université de Montréal. He received his B.A. and M.A. degrees, in sociology, from the Université de Montréal and his Ph.D. from the Université La Sorbonne and the École des Hautes Études en Sciences Sociales of Paris. In 1970, Dr. Maheu joined the sociology faculty of the Université de Montréal. He was a visiting scholar in many universities and countries including Great Britain, Italy, Brazil, France, Germany, China, and the United States. Dr. Maheu is author, co-author or editor of books, journals, and numerous scientific articles on social movements, social classes, scientific organizations, communities, and universities. His latest work, supported by the Social Sciences and Humanities Research Council and the Quebec Fund for Research and Training (FCAR), pertains to the institutionalization of collective action and social movements within late modern institutions and societies. Dr. Maheu has served on and chaired many committees concerned with higher education, research, and graduate education related to the Canadian Association for Graduate Studies, the Quebec Council of Universities, the Quebec Association of Graduate Deans, the Canadian Foundation for the Social Sciences, the International Sociological Association, and the International Bureau of Sociology. He also has been a member of advisory committees and review panels of the Social Sciences and Humanities Research Council and the Ontario Council of Graduate Studies. Dr. Maheu is currently the Chair of the Research Committee of the Board of the Centre Hospitalier de l'Université de Montréal (CHUM) and is a member of the Canadian Institute for Advanced Research Council. Dr. Maheu also served on the Panel on Reputational Measures and Data Presentation.

LAWRENCE MARTIN, Ph.D., is Dean of the Graduate School and Associate Provost for Analysis and Planning at Stony Brook University. He received his Ph.D. in anthropology from University College London in 1983 and was a Postdoctoral Fellow in anatomy at University College London until 1985. Dr. Martin joined the Departments of Anthropology and Anatomical Sciences at Stony Brook in 1985. He served as Director of Undergraduate Studies and Director of the Doctoral Program in Anthropological Sciences before his appointment as Dean of the Graduate School in 1993. Dr. Martin's anthropological research interests focus on species recognition in fossil primates, evolution of apes and humans, and microstructure and development of dental enamel in primates. He has analyzed the data from the 1995 research-doctorate study to assess programs at his own institution and to understand the relationship between the different measures used in that study across all programs in a number of fields. He also served on the Panel on Quantitative Measures and the Panel on Reputational Measures and Data Presentation.

MARESI NERAD, Ph.D., is Director of the National Center for Innovation and Research in Graduate Education (CIRGE), Associate Dean of the Graduate School, and Research Associate Professor for Educational Leadership and Policy Studies in the College of Education at the University of Washington. She received a doctorate in higher education from the University of California-Berkeley in 1988. From 1988 to 2000, Dr. Nerad directed research in the Graduate Division at the University of California-Berkeley and spent the 2000 to 2001 academic year as Dean in Residence at the Council of Graduate Schools. She is the author or editor of three books on women, women studies in the U.S., and on U.S. graduate education. Dr. Nerad's current research and publications focus on many aspects of graduate and postdoctoral education across major disciplines, including issues of class, race, gender, and citizenship. Dr. Nerad's most recent work (two national studies entitled *Ph.D.s-10 Years Later* and *Ph.D.s in Art History—Over a Decade Later*) is directly related to this study. She also served on the Panel on Student Processes and Outcomes.

FRANK SOLOMON, Ph.D., is a Professor of Biology at Massachusetts Institute of Technology (MIT). He received his B.A. in history from Harvard University in 1964 and his Ph.D. in biochemistry in 1970 from Brandeis University. Following his doctorate he held a Postdoctoral Fellowship at Philadelphia's Institute for Cancer Research and lived in Switzerland, where he developed his interest in cell biology. Dr. Solomon joined the faculty at MIT in 1974. His research focuses on the intracellular determinants of differentiated cell morphology and the mechanisms of their expression—i.e., how cells organize their cytoplasm to produce differentiated morphology and motility. Dr. Solomon has a strong interest in graduate education and served as Chair of the American Society of Cell Biology Education Committee. He also served as co-chair of the Panel on Taxonomy and Interdisciplinarity.

CATHARINE R. STIMPSON, Ph.D., is Dean of the Graduate School of Arts and Science, and University Professor at New York University. She earned an A.B. in English, *magna cum laude*, from Bryn Mawr College in 1958; a B.A. with honors in 1960 and an M.A. in 1966 from Newnham College, Cambridge University; and a Ph.D. with distinction from Columbia University in 1967. Dr. Stimpson was a member of the English Department of Barnard College (1963-80), where she was the first director of the Women's Center and the founding editor of *SIGNS: JOURNAL OF WOMEN IN CULTURE AND SOCIETY* (1974-80) for the University of Chicago Press. In 1980, she became Professor of English at Rutgers University, then Dean of the Graduate School, Vice Provost for Graduate Education, and University Professor; she was also the first director of the Institute for Research on Women. While continuing to teach at Rutgers, Dr. Stimpson also served as Director of the MacArthur Foundation Fellows Program (1994-97). She is a former chair of the New York State Humanities Council and the National Council for Research on Women as well as past president of the Modern Language Association. Dr. Stimpson also served as president of the Association of Graduate Schools in 2000-01 and is currently on the board of the Council of Graduate Schools. She holds honorary degrees from several universities and colleges, including Bates, Hamilton, and the University of Arizona. Dr. Stimpson's publications include a book, *Where the Meanings Are: Feminism and Cultural Spaces,* and a novel, *Class Notes.* She has edited seven books, has served as co-editor of the Library of America's *Gertrude Stein: Writings 1903-1932* and *Gertrude Stein: Writings 1932-1946,* and has published over 150 monographs, essays, stories, and reviews. Dr. Stimpson also served as the Chair of the Panel on Quantitative Measures.

PANEL ON TAXONOMY AND INTERDISCIPLINARITY

Biosketches

WALTER COHEN, Ph.D., *Co-Chair,* is currently Vice Provost and Professor of Comparative Literature at Cornell University and the former Dean of the Graduate School. He did his undergraduate work at Stanford University. After earning his Ph.D. from the University of California-Berkeley in 1980, Dr. Cohen joined the Cornell faculty. His academic specialties are Renaissance drama and literary theory. Dr. Cohen served as president of the Association of Graduate Schools from 1998 to1999. Dr. Cohen is a member of the parent committee for this panel.

FRANK SOLOMON, Ph.D., *Co-Chair,* is a Professor of Biology at the Massachusetts Institute of Technology (MIT). He received his B.A. in history from Harvard University in 1964 and his Ph.D. in biochemistry in 1970 from Brandeis University. He was a postdoctoral fellow at the Institute for Cancer Research in Philadelphia, and a research associate at Friedrich Miescher Institute in Basel, Switzerland, where he conducted research in cell biology. He joined the MIT faculty in 1974. His research focuses on the intracellular determinants of differentiated cell morphology and the mechanisms of their expression: how cells organize their cytoplasm to produce differentiated morphology and motility. Dr. Solomon has received awards for his teaching and mentoring at MIT and serves as Chair of the American Society of Cell Biology Education Committee. Dr. Solomon is a member of the parent committee for this panel.

GEORGE BUGLIARELLO, Sc.D. (NAE), is President Emeritus and University Professor at Polytechnic University, where he served as President (1973-94) and Chancellor (1994-2003). He holds a Dott. Ing. in 1951 from the University of Padua, an M.S. in 1954 from the University of Minnesota, and a Sc.D. in 1959 from Massachusetts Institute of Technology. Dr. Bugliarello has a range of administrative experience as professor and dean of engineering at the University of Illinois at Chicago Circle and as professor and chairman of the Biotechnology Program at Carnegie Mellon University. His honors and awards include: Member of the National Academy of Engineering (NAE), Founding Fellow of the American Institute for Medical and Biological Engineering, Fellow of the American Society for Engineering Education, Fellow of the American Society of Civil Engineers, and Fellow of the New York Academy of Sciences. Dr. Bugliarello is Past President of Sigma Xi—the Scientific Research Society, and was elected in 2003 to a four-year term as Foreign Secretary of the NAE. His research interests include biomedical engineering, fluid mechanics, computer languages, and socio-technology. Dr. Bugliarello is a member of the parent committee for this panel.

ELTON D. ABERLE, Ph.D., is Dean of the College of Agricultural and Life Sciences at the University of Wisconsin-Madison. He received his B.S. from Kansas State University in 1962, his M.S. from Michigan State University in 1965, and his Ph.D. from Michigan State University in food sciences in 1967. Previously, Dr. Aberle held administrative positions at the University of Nebraska-Lincoln's Institute of Agriculture and Natural Resources, and a faculty position at Purdue University. His research and teaching background is in muscle and adipose tissue growth, meat quality and meat processing. Dr. Aberle has taught courses in meat science, animal growth and food chemistry. He is a member of the parent committee for this panel.

ROBERT F. JONES, Ph.D., is Vice President for Institutional and Faculty Studies at the Association of American Medical Colleges. His division is responsible for addressing strategic and management policy questions for academic medical centers, and the maintenance of several major AAMC databases, including the Institutional Profile System, the Faculty Salary Survey, and the Faculty Roster. Dr. Jones's research on medical school issues focuses on institutional organization, governance, and management, faculty personnel policies, tenure, faculty compensation, medical school financing, and the cost of medical education. He has served as a consultant to the National Science Foundation, the National Institutes of Health, the National Research Council as well as numerous other organizations and institutions.

LEONARD K. PETERS, Ph.D., is Vice Provost for Research at Virginia Polytechnic Institute and State University. Previously, he served as Department Chair, Associate Dean in the Graduate School, Vice Chancellor for Research and Graduate Studies, and Acting Vice President for Research and Graduate Studies at the University of Kentucky. His academic training and background are in chemical engineering with B.S., M.S., and Ph.D. degrees all from the University of Pittsburgh. Dr. Peters' research and teaching interests are in regional and global-scale atmospheric chemistry and pollution. He has served on a number of councils and boards, including Oak Ridge Associated Universities where he is past chair of the Board of Directors, the Southeastern Universities Research Association, the Southern Technology Council. Dr. Peters was chair of the Council of Graduate Schools Board of Directors.

RICHARD ATTIYEH, Ph.D., is Vice Chancellor for Research and Dean of Graduate Studies as well as Professor of Economics at the University of California, San Diego. He had also served as chair, and later dean, of the Department of Economics. Prior to his appointment at UCSD in 1967, Dr. Attiyeh served as staff economist for the President's

Council of Economic Advisors and as an assistant professor at Stanford and Yale. He was also past chair of the Graduate Record Examinations (GRE) Board and the Council of Graduate Schools' (CGS) Board of Directors, and past president of the Association of Graduate Schools (AGS). Dr. Attiyeh is the current chair of the Executive Committee of the AAU/AGS Project for Research on Doctoral Education and the Chairman of the Board of Directors of the California Biomedical Research Association.

PANEL ON QUANTITATIVE MEASURES

Biosketches

CATHARINE R. STIMPSON, Ph.D., *Chair,* is Dean of the Graduate School of Arts and Science, and University Professor at New York University. She earned an A.B. in English, *magna cum laude*, from Bryn Mawr College in 1958; a B.A. with honors in 1960 and an M.A. in 1966 from Newnham College, Cambridge University; and a Ph.D. with distinction from Columbia University in 1967. Formerly, Dr. Stimpson was a member of the English Department of Barnard College (1963-80), where she was the first director of the Women's Center and the founding editor of *SIGNS: JOURNAL OF WOMEN IN CULTURE AND SOCIETY* (1974-80) for the University of Chicago Press. In 1980, she became Professor of English at Rutgers University, then Dean of the Graduate School, Vice Provost for Graduate Education, and University Professor; she was also the first director of the Institute for Research on Women. While continuing to teach at Rutgers, Dr. Stimpson also served as Director of the MacArthur Foundation Fellows Program (1994-97). She is a former chair of the New York State Humanities Council and the National Council for Research on Women as well as past president of the Modern Language Association. Dr. Stimpson also served as president of the Association of Graduate Schools in 2000-01 and is currently on the board of the Council of Graduate Schools. She holds honorary degrees from several universities and colleges, including Bates, Hamilton, and the University of Arizona. Dr. Stimpson's publications include a book, *Where the Meanings Are: Feminism and Cultural Spaces,* and a novel, *Class Notes.* She has edited seven books, has served as co-editor of the Library of America's *Gertrude Stein: Writings 1903-1932* and *Gertrude Stein: Writings 1932-1946,* and has published over 150 monographs, essays, stories, and reviews. She also serves on the parent committee for this panel.

RONALD GRAHAM, Ph.D., is Irwin and Joan Jacobs Professor in the Department of Computer Science and Engineering at the University of California-San Diego and Chief Scientist at the California Institute for Telecommunication and Information Technology of the University of California-San Diego. He holds an M.A. and a Ph.D. in mathematics from the University of California-Berkeley as well as a B.S.

in physics from the University of Alaska at Fairbanks. Dr. Graham served as Director of Information Sciences at AT&T Bell Laboratories for more than 30 years. He has held numerous professorships in mathematics and computer science at institutions such as Rutgers University, Princeton University, Stanford University, and the California Institute of Technology. Dr. Graham's research work focuses on topics such as worst-case analysis in scheduling theory, on-line algorithms and amortized analysis in the Graham's scan in computational geometry, Ramsey Theory, and quasi-randomness. He has served on numerous NAS boards and committees. Dr. Graham is a member of the National Academy of Sciences and serves as NAS Treasurer. He is a Past President of the American Mathematical Society and currently serves as President of the Mathematical Association of America. He is a member of the parent committee for this panel.

MARSHA KELMAN, M.B.A., is the Associate Vice President and Director of the Office of Institutional Studies, and an adjunct faculty member in the Higher Education Administration Program at the University of Texas at Austin (UT). She has been active in professional associations at the state, regional, and national levels, including terms as an officer in the Texas Association for Institutional Research (TAIR), the Southern Association for Institutional Research (SAIR), and the Association for Institutional Research (AIR). She is the recipient of outstanding service awards from both TAIR and SAIR. She has served on advisory committees on matters concerning data policy for the National Postsecondary Education Cooperative, the National Center for Education Statistics, the National Science Foundation, and the Texas Higher Education Coordinating Board. She has been the Association of American Universities (AAU) Data Exchange representative for UT Austin since 1982, and is a member and chair of the council for this group. She has chaired numerous working groups focusing on improving aspects of the data exchange and is currently a member of the consistency and quality taskforce and of the data warehouse development taskforce. She also served on the technical advisory group to the AAU Membership Committee in 1999-2000.

LAWRENCE MARTIN, Ph.D., is Dean of the Graduate School and Associate Provost for Analysis and Planning at Stony Brook University. He received his Ph.D. in anthropology from University College London in 1983 and was a Postdoctoral Fellow in anatomy at University College London until 1985. Dr. Martin joined the Departments of Anthropology and Anatomical Sciences at Stony Brook in 1985. He served as Director of Undergraduate Studies and Director of the Doctoral Program in Anthropological Sciences before his appointment as Dean of the Graduate School in 1993. Dr. Martin's anthropological research interests focus on species recognition in fossil primates, evolution of apes and humans, and microstructure and development of dental enamel in primates. He has analyzed the data from the 1995 research-doctorate study to assess programs at his own institution and to understand the relationship between the different measures used in that study across all programs in a number of fields. He is a member of the parent committee for this panel.

JEREMIAH P. OSTRIKER, Ph.D. (NAS), is a professor of astrophysical sciences at Princeton University and Plumian Professor of Astronomy and Experimental Philosophy at the University of Cambridge. He received his B.A. in physics and chemistry from Harvard University and his Ph.D. in astrophysics from the University of Chicago. After a postdoctoral fellowship at Cambridge University, Dr. Ostriker served on the faculty at Princeton University as a professor (1966-present), as department chair and director of the Princeton University Observatory (1979-1995), and as university provost (1995-2001). During his tenure as provost, Princeton received a major grant from the Mellon Foundation to improve doctoral education in the humanities. He has received many awards and honors, including membership in the National Academy of Sciences (NAS) and in 2001, the U.S. National Medal of Science. He has served on several National Research Council (NRC) and National Academies committees, including the NAS Council and the NRC Governing Board. Dr. Ostriker also serves as the chair of the parent committee for this panel.

CHARLES E. PHELPS, Ph.D., is Provost and Professor of Political Science and Economics at the University of Rochester. At the University of Rochester he was director of the Public Policy Analysis Program, Chair of the Department of Community and Preventive Medicine in the School of Medicine and Dentistry. Formerly, Dr. Phelps was at the RAND Corporation as Staff Economist, Senior Staff Economist, and Director of the Program on Regulatory Policies and Institutions; he studied issues related to health policy, natural resources and environmental policy, and energy policy, and helped to found the RAND Health Insurance Experiment. He was elected to the Institute of Medicine in 1991. Dr. Phelps served from 1990 - 1994 as a peer reviewer for grant applications to the Agency for Health Care Policy and Research of the United States government. He has been associate editor of four professional journals (currently Journal of Health Economics, and the Economics Bulletin, and previously the Journal of Policy Analysis and Management, and Journal of Risk and Uncertainty), and served 3 years as a Trustee for the Society for Medical Decision Making. He has published over 50 peer-reviewed papers and manuscripts, and a textbook, Health Economics, now in its third edition (2002). Locally, Phelps served as a founding member of the Rochester Health Commission. Professor Phelps's research focuses on issues related to scholarly communication and digital technology.

PETER SYVERSON, M.S., is Vice President for Research and Information Services at the Council of Graduate Schools. He has been involved in the higher education policy community in Washington for the past two decades. He is responsible for the research activities of the Council, which include directing the national CGS/GRE Survey of Graduate Enrollment, the preparation of reports and articles that summarize CGS data, other research that bears on graduate education, and representing the Council on a number of advisory committees involved in the conduct of national studies of U.S. higher education. He began his career in 1975 at the National Academy of Sciences where he directed the Survey of Earned Doctorates, the national survey of all new doctorate recipients. As Project Director, Peter worked to transform the annual *Summary Report* from a set of statistical highlights to a policy-research document. He led the project through the transition from a paper-based questionnaire processing system to a computer-based system. At the Council of Graduate Schools he established the Council's first office of research and working with the GRE Board, he developed a new Survey of Graduate Enrollment. That survey, now in its tenth year, has become a respected source of information on trends in graduate enrollment and application for graduate study. His primary research interests involve the flow of individuals into and through graduate education and the labor market experiences of advanced-degree recipients.

PANEL ON REPUTATIONAL MEASURES AND DATA PRESENTATION

Biosketches

JONATHAN COLE, Ph.D., *Co-Chair*, is the John Mitchell Mason Professor of the University and Provost at Columbia University. He joined the faculty at Columbia in 1968 and served as the Director of the Center for Social Sciences from 1979 to 1987, Vice Provost for Arts and Sciences from 1987 to 1989, and the Quetelet Professor of Social Sciences from 1989 to 2001. Dr. Cole's awards and honors include a Guggenheim Fellowship, Fellow of the Center of Advanced Study in the Behavioral Sciences, and Fellow of the American Academy of Arts and Sciences. He has published extensively on the growth of scientific knowledge, the social organization of peer review in science, and women in the scientific community. Dr. Cole was a member of the previous committee for the study of research-doctorate programs and serves on the current parent committee for this panel.

PAUL HOLLAND, Ph.D., *Co-Chair*, holds the Frederic M. Lord Chair in Measurement and Statistics and is acting director of the Center for Statistical Theory and Practice at the Educational Testing Service (ETS). He earned a B.A. in mathematics from the University of Michigan, and an M.A. and a Ph.D. in statistics from Stanford University. Dr. Holland's association with ETS began in 1975 as

Director of the Research Statistics Group. In 1986, he was appointed ETS's first Distinguished Research Scientist. In 1993, Dr. Holland joined the faculty at University of California-Berkeley as a professor in the Graduate School of Education and the Department of Statistics, but returned in 2000 to his current position at ETS. His research interests include psychometrics, causal inference of educational interventions in non-experimental studies; multivariate analysis and the explanation of score scales. He serves on the parent committee for this panel.

JOHN BRAUMAN, Ph.D. (NAS), is the J.G. Jackson-C.J. Jackson Professor of Chemistry and Cognizant Dean for the Natural Sciences at Stanford University. He received his B.S. in 1959 from the Massachusetts Institute of Technology and his Ph.D. in 1963 from the University of California-Berkeley. Dr. Brauman's research is directed toward understanding how molecules react and the factors that determine the rates and products of chemical reactions. The principal areas of his research involve the spectroscopy, photochemistry, reaction dynamics, and reaction mechanisms of ions in the gas phase. Dr. Brauman is a member of the National Academy of Sciences (NAS), a Fellow of the American Academy of Arts and Sciences as well as of the American Association for the Advancement of Science, and an Honorary Fellow of the California Academy of Sciences. He has received numerous honors, including an NAS Award in the Chemical Sciences and an American Chemical Society award in Pure Chemistry. In his role as Cognizant Dean he oversees the departments of: applied physics, biological sciences, history, mathematics, physics, psychology, statistics, and the Hopkins Marine Station. He also serves on the parent committee for this panel.

LOUIS MAHEU, Ph.D., is Dean and Vice President of Graduate Studies of the Université de Montréal. He received his B.A. and M.A. degrees, in sociology, from the Université de Montréal and his Ph.D. from the Université La Sorbonne and the École des Hautes Études en Sciences Sociales of Paris. In 1970, Dr. Maheu joined the sociology faculty of the Université de Montréal. He was a visiting scholar in many universities and countries including Great Britain, Italy, Brazil, France, Germany, China and the United States. Dr. Maheu is author, co-author or editor of books, journals and numerous scientific articles on social movements, social classes, scientific organizations, communities, and universities. His latest work, supported by the Social Sciences and Humanities Research Council and the Quebec Fund for Research and Training (FCAR), pertains to the institutionalization of collective action and social movements within late modern institutions and societies. Dr. Maheu has served on and chaired many committees concerned with higher education, research and graduate education related to the Canadian Association for Graduate Studies, the Quebec Council of Universities, the Quebec Association of Graduate Deans, the

Canadian Foundation for the Social Sciences, the International Sociological Association and the International Bureau of Sociology. He also has been a member of advisory committees and review panels of the Social Sciences and Humanities Research Council and the Ontario Council of Graduate Studies. Dr. Maheu is currently the Chair of the Research Committee of the Board of the Centre Hospitalier de l'Université de Montréal (CHUM) and is a member of the Canadian Institute for Advanced Research Council. Dr. Maheu is also a member of the parent committee for this panel.

LAWRENCE MARTIN, Ph.D., is Dean of the Graduate School and Associate Provost for Analysis and Planning at Stony Brook University. He received his Ph.D. in anthropology from University College London in 1983 and was a Postdoctoral Fellow in anatomy at University College London until 1985. Dr. Martin joined the Departments of Anthropology and Anatomical Sciences at Stony Brook in 1985. He served as Director of Undergraduate Studies and Director of the Doctoral Program in Anthropological Sciences before his appointment as Dean of the Graduate School in 1993. Dr. Martin's anthropological research interests focus on species recognition in fossil primates, evolution of apes and humans, and microstructure and development of dental enamel in primates. He has analyzed the data from the 1995 research-doctorate study to assess programs at his own institution and to understand the relationship between the different measures used in that study across all programs in a number of fields. He also serves on the parent committee for this panel.

DAVID SCHMIDLY, Ph.D., became the 13th President of Texas Tech University in 2000, after joining the university in 1996 in a dual role of Vice President for Research and Graduate Studies and Dean of the Graduate School. In 1999, his duties were expanded to include responsibility for technology transfer activities. He also served on the faculty and administration of Texas A&M University for 25 years, including five years as CEO and Campus Dean of the Galveston campus and six years as head of the Department of Wildlife and Fisheries Sciences at College Station. He earned his B.A. and M.A. from Texas Tech and a Ph.D. from the University of Illinois. Dr. Schmidly is a biologist, specializing in systematics, taxonomy, and natural history of mammals. He is also a specialist in natural resource management and conversation. He has authored more than 100 scientific papers and seven books. Dr. Schmidly's latest book, *Texas Natural History: A Century of Change,* was published by the Texas Tech University Press in April 2002.

DONALD RUBIN, Ph.D., is Chair and Professor of Statistics at Harvard University. He earned his B.A. from Princeton University in 1965 and his Ph.D. from Harvard University in 1970. Dr. Rubin's research interests include inference in sample surveys with nonresponse and missing data problems, and developing and applying statistical models to data in a variety of scientific disciplines. He is a member of the American Academy of Arts and Sciences, a Fellow of the Institute of Mathematical Statistics, American Association for the Advancement of Science, and the American Statistical Association (ASA). The ASA awarded Dr. Rubin with the S.S. Wilkes Medal as well as the Parzen Prize. He was also a Guggenheim Fellow from 1977-78.

PANEL ON STUDENT PROCESSES AND OUTCOMES

Biosketches

JOAN F. LORDEN, Ph.D., is Provost and Vice Chancellor for Academic Affairs at the University of North Carolina at Charlotte. She received a B.A. from the City College of New York and a Ph.D. from Yale University. Dr. Lorden served for over eight years as Dean of the Graduate School and Associate Provost for Research at the University of Alabama at Birmingham (UAB). During 2002-03, she was the Council of Graduate Schools (CGS) Dean-in-Residence at the Division of Graduate Education at the National Science Foundation and chaired the CGS Board of Directors. Dr. Lorden's research focuses on brain-behavior relationships. At UAB she organized the doctoral program in behavioral neuroscience and was a founding member and director of the university-wide interdisciplinary Graduate Training Program in Neuroscience. As Graduate Dean, Dr. Lorden fostered programs that increased opportunities for breadth of training among graduate students and served as the program director for an interdisciplinary biological sciences training grant. Throughout her tenure as graduate dean, she was actively involved in programs designed to improve the recruitment of women and minorities into doctoral programs in science and engineering, and received several grants to advance these goals. She is also a member of the parent committee for this panel.

ELTON D. ABERLE, Ph.D., is Dean of the College of Agricultural and Life Sciences at the University of Wisconsin-Madison. He received his B.S. from Kansas State University in 1962, his M.S. from Michigan State University in 1965, and his Ph.D. from Michigan State University in food sciences in 1967. Previously, Dr. Aberle held administrative positions at the University of Nebraska-Lincoln's Institute of Agriculture and Natural Resources, and a faculty position at Purdue University. His research and teaching background is in muscle biology, and animal and food sciences. Dr. Aberle has received teaching and research awards from the American Society of Animal Sciences and the American Meat Science Association, and is a Fellow of the American Association for the Advancement of Science and the American Society of Animal Science. Dr. Aberle is a member of the parent committee for this panel.

ADAM FAGEN is a doctoral candidate in Molecular Biology and Education at Harvard University and expects to complete his degree in 2002. He helped to direct the National Doctoral Program Survey of the National Association of Graduate-Professional Students. Mr. Fagen has held teaching fellow positions since 1995 and was head fellow in the principles of physics and mechanics course at Harvard. He currently serves as coordinator of the Research Experience for Teachers Program. Mr. Fagen holds an M.A. in Molecular and Cellular Biology from Harvard and a B.A. (with Distinction) from Swarthmore. He is a recipient of an NSF graduate fellowship. Mr. Fagen brings to this panel the knowledge he gained from work on the National Doctoral Program Survey of the National Association of Graduate-Professional Students as well as his perspective on doctoral education as a current student.

GEORGE KUH, Ph.D., is Chancellor's Professor of Higher Education at Indiana University Bloomington. He directs the College Student Experiences Questionnaire Research Program and the National Survey of Student Engagement, which is sponsored by The Carnegie Foundation for the Advancement of Teaching and supported by the Lumina Foundation for Education and The Pew Charitable Trusts. Dr. Kuh taught at Kirkwood Community College and the University of Iowa Colleges of Education and Dentistry and was a visiting professor at Iowa State University and Portland State University. At Indiana University, he served as chairperson of the Department of Educational Leadership and Policy Studies (1982-84), Associate Dean for Academic Affairs in the School of Education (1985-88), and Associate Dean of the Faculties for the Bloomington campus (1997-2000). Dr. Kuh has more than 200 publications and has made several hundred presentations on topics related to college student development, assessment strategies for post-secondary programs and environments, and campus cultures. His recent research and scholarly activities have focused on assessing student learning and personal development, campus cultures, out-of-class experiences of undergraduates, and the institutional conditions that foster student learning.

EARL LEWIS, Ph.D., is Dean of the Graduate School, Vice Provost for Academic Affairs-Graduate Studies, and the Elsa Barkley Brown and Robin D.G. Kelley Collegiate Professor of History and African-American Studies at the University of Michigan. He earned his undergraduate degree from Concordia College in Moorhead, Minnesota, where he majored in history and psychology, and earned his doctorate in history at the University of Minnesota. Dr. Lewis's first academic appointment was at the University of California-Berkeley, where he taught from 1984-89. He is past Chair of the Board of the Council of Graduate Schools, a member of the GRE Board, and National Chair of the Responsive Ph.D. project. Dr. Lewis is the author or editor of five books, including *In Their Own Interests: Race, Class and Power in Twentieth-Century Norfolk*. His awards include the Gustavus

Myers Outstanding Book Award for the co-edited volume, *To Make Our World Anew*, and the *Chicago Tribune's* favorite book for 2001 recognition for *Love on Trial*. Dr. Lewis is a member of the parent committee for this panel.

MARESI NERAD, Ph.D., is Director of the National Center for Innovation and Research in Graduate Education (CIRGE), Associate Dean of the Graduate School, and Research Associate Professor for Educational Leadership and Policy Studies in the College of Education at the University of Washington. She received a doctorate in higher education from the University of California-Berkeley in 1988. From 1988 to 2000, Dr. Nerad directed research in the Graduate Division at the University of California-Berkeley and spent the 2000 to 2001 academic year as Dean in Residence at the Council of Graduate Schools. She is the author or editor of three books on women, women studies in the U.S., and on U.S. graduate education. Dr. Nerad's current research and publications focus on many aspects of graduate and postdoctoral education across major disciplines, including issues of class, race, gender, and citizenship. Dr. Nerad's most recent work (two national studies entitled *Ph.D.s-10 Years Later* and *Ph.D.s in Art History—Over a Decade Later*) is directly related to this study. Dr. Nerad is a member of the parent committee for this panel.

BRENDA RUSSELL, Ph.D., is Professor of Physiology and Biophysics, Bioengineering and Medicine and Associate Vice Chancellor for Research at the University of Illinois at Chicago since 1988. She did research into muscle biology in the colleges of medicine at Duke, UCLA, and Rush University. Dr. Russell is active in research with NIH funding and has served on study sections for NIH and the American Heart Association. She is past president of the GREAT (Graduate Research Education and Teaching) Group of the American Association of Medical Colleges. She is former editor of *The American Journal of Physiology Cell* Section; *Cell & Tissue Research* and editorial board member of many journals, including *Circulation Research* and *The Journal of Applied Physiology*. Dr. Russell has written reviews, book chapters and over 100 publications in peer-reviewed journals.

SUSANNA RYAN, Ph.D., received her B.A. in literature from Sarah Lawrence College (1989) and her M.A. (1997) and Ph.D. (2002) in English Language and Literature from the University of Michigan. She has received numerous fellowships from the Rackham Graduate School at the University of Michigan as well as awards from the Andrew W. Mellon Foundation and the Yale Center for British Art. Dr. Ryan is the currently a Woodrow Wilson Postdoctoral Fellow in the Humanities at Indiana University. Prior to her graduate career, she taught English at the Ethel Walker School, an all-girls secondary school in Connecticut. Dr. Ryan has published several articles and is currently revising her dissertation for publication (*Coming to the Whip: Horsemanship and the Politics of Victorian Empathy*).

Appendix B

Program-Initiation Consultation with Organizations

GROUPS CONSULTED IN CONNECTION WITH THE PREPARATION OF THE PROPOSAL TO CONDUCT A METHODOLOGY STUDY FOR THE ASSESSMENT OF RESEARCH-DOCTORATE PROGRAMS

American Academy of Arts and Sciences:	Metrics in the Humanities Project
Association of American Universities:	Meetings of Chief Academic Officers, Arts and Sciences Deans
Conference of Southern Graduates Schools	
Council of Graduate Schools:	Annual Meeting
National Academy of Sciences:	Regional members meetings, chemistry section meeting, Committee on Science Engineering and Public Policy, Commission on the Behavioral and Social Sciences and Education
National Association of State Universities and Land Grant Colleges:	Committee on Research Policy and Graduate Education
Northeastern Association of Graduate Schools	
U.S. Department of Education	Leadership Summit on Diversity in Doctoral Education
Campus visits:	University of California, Berkeley University of California, Davis Purdue University Virginia Polytechnic Institution and State University

Professional Societies:

American Academy of Kinesiology and Physical Education
American Academy of Religion
American Society for Microbiology
American Institute of Physics
American Chemical Society
American Society for Nutritional Sciences
American Mathematical Society
American Society for Engineering Education
Association of American Medical Colleges
Federation of American Societies of Experimental Biology
National Association of Graduate and Professional Students
Council of Communications Associations
University Corporation for Atmospheric Research

PROFESSIONAL SOCIETIES CONTACTED

1. Acoustical Society of America	Charles Schmid, Executive Director
2. African Studies Association	Loree Jones, Executive Director
3. American Academy of Religion	Barbara DeConcini, Executive Director
4. American Anthropological Association	Bill Davis, Executive Director
5. American Association for Agricultural Education	
6. American Association of Anatomists	Andrea Pendleton, Executive Director
7. American Association of Immunologists	M. Michele. Hogan, Executive Director
8. American Association of Pharmaceutical Scientists	John Cox, Executive Director
9. American Association of Physical Anthropologists	Martin Nickels, Edu. Comm. Chair
10. American Chemical Society	John Crum, Executive Director
11. American College of Neuropsychopharmacology	Ronnie Wilkins, Executive Director
12. American Comparative Literature Association	
13. American Economic Association	John Siegfried, Secretary Treasurer
14. American Genetic Association	Stephen O'Brien, Editor
15. American Historical Association	Anita Jones, Executive Director
16. American Institute of Biological Sciences	Richard O'Grady, Executive Director
17. American Institute of Chemists	Jill Clawson, Executive Director
18. American Institute of Physics	Marc Brodsky, Executive Director
19. American Mathematical Society	John Ewing, Executive Director
20. American Meteorological Society	Ronald McPherson, Executive Director
21. American Musicological Society	Robert Judd, Executive Director
22. American Nuclear Society	Harry Bradley, Executive Director
23. American Pharmaceutical Association	John Gans, Executive Director
24. Academy of Pharmaceutical Research and Science	
25. American Philological Association	Adam Blistein, Executive Director
26. American Philosophical Society	Mary Dunn, Executive Director
27. American Physical Society	Judy Franz, Executive Director
28. American Political Science Association	Michael Brintnall, Executive Director
29. American Psychological Association	Raymond Fowler, Executive Director
30. American Psychological Society	Alan Kraut, Executive Director
31. American Society for Aesthetics	Curtis Carter, Executive Director
32. American Society for Biochemistry and Molecular Biology	Charles Hancock, Executive Director
33. American Society for Horticultural Science	Michael Neff, Executive Director
34. American Society for Information Science and Technology	Richard Hill, Executive Director
34. American Society for Investigative Pathology	Mark Sobel, Executive Director
35. American Society for Microbiology	Michael Goldberg, Executive Director
36. American Society for Nutritional Sciences	Richard Allison, Executive Director
37. American Society for Theatre Research	Judy Wilmeth, Record Keeper
38. American Society of Agronomy	Luther Smith, Executive Director
39. American Society of Animal Science	Ellen G. M. Bergfeld, Executive Director
40. American Society of Criminology	Chris Eskridge, Executive Director
41. American Society of Human Genetics	Joann Boughman, Executive Director
42. American Society of Limnology and Oceanography	Phinney Jonathan, Executive Director Oceanography
43. American Society Plant Physiologists	John Lisack, Jr., Executive Director
44. American Sociological Association	Sally Hillsman, Executive Director
45. American Statistical Association	Pat McClellan, Executive Director
46. Association for Computing Machinery	John White, Executive Director
47. Association for Women in Science	Catherine Didion, Executive Director
48. Association of American Geographers	Ronald Able, Executive Director
49. Biophysical Society	Rosalba Kampman, Executive Director
50. Botanical Society of America	Jeffrey Osborn, Executive Director

Appendix C

Meetings and Participants

1. Program Initiation: Planning Meeting and Participants, June 1999
2. Meeting Schedule of Parent Committee and Four Panels
   - Agendas of All Committee and Panel Meetings

PLANNING MEETING PROGRAM

Tuesday, June 22, 1999

8:30 AM
Welcome
    M. R. C. Greenwood, University of California, Santa Cruz

8:45 AM
Introductory Remarks

9:00 AM
A. Why Do Another Research-Doctorate Study

The reactions to the past two studies of Research-Doctorate Programs by the NRC were both positive and negative. Some institutions were critical of the objective and/or subjective measures used to characterize their programs, but at the same time they found the data from the studies and the rankings of their programs useful in conducting their own analyses and assessments. The rationale for doing another study lies in finding better measures to describe doctoral programs and to collect data on these measures that will better serve institutions and doctoral education. Some general issues that should guide the design and implementation of the next study are:

- *The value derived by educational institutions from the results of past studies.*
- *The relevance of the data from past studies to the mission of educational programs.*
- *The use of objective measures to support the reputational ratings and vise versa.*
- *Balancing the measurement of the quality of the research faculty and the effectiveness of the educational program.*

This opening session will address these and other general issues.

Presenters: Jules LaPidus, Council of Graduate Schools
                     Stanley Ikenberry, American Council for Education
                     Joseph Bordogna, National Science Foundation

10:45 AM
B. Value and Purpose of Program Assessments: Users and Insight

The audience for research-doctorate reports has expanded over time. While it is primarily used by universities in planning their academic programs, researchers have used the ratings and the objective measures to analyze different aspects of doctoral education, government agencies used the data to develop programs and allocating resources, and students use the rankings to select programs for graduate study. Understanding how the study is used and what measures are of interest to different groups would assist in guiding the design of the next study.

Presenters: Lawrence Martin, State University of New York, Stony Brook
                     Lesley Lydell, University of Minnesota
                     Gary Walters, Ohio State Board of Regents

1:00 PM
C. Assessing Quality: Validity and Importance of Reputational Measures

Some of the criticisms of past research-doctorate studies have been directed at the over emphasis placed on the reputational measures and inconsistencies between these measures and objective measures. Neither changing the reputational measures for the last study nor using a different methodology for the Survey of Graduate Faculty were considered in order to gain consistency with the 1982 study. This session will try to place in perspective the role of reputational measures in measuring the quality of programs and to determine ways in which this measure can be enhanced.

Presenters: Brendan Maher, Harvard University
                     Jonathan Cole, Columbia University

2:00 PM
D. Assessing Quality: Through Objective Measures

In addition to reputational measures, data on publication, research grants, and awards have also been used in past study to assess the quality of programs. The measures for assessing faculty quality have been improved over successive studies, but they are still over shadowed by the reputational measures. How can these measures be improved to better represent the quality of the research-doctoral programs, and how can these measures, together with the reputational measures, be analyzed and presented to give a more informed estimate of program quality? The introduction of new measures will also be a major focus of the next study.

Presenters: Stephen Stigler, University of Chicago
                     Hugh Graham, Vanderbilt University

3:15 PM
E. Finding the Right Field Taxonomy

Since the basis for the study is the identification of programs within an institution, independent of the academic unit which houses the program, it is important to find a taxonomy and a means for identifying programs that are consistent across all institutions. Not having a well defined taxonomy results in incomplete faculty rosters, misinterpretations of program content, incomplete field coverage, and in general the possible assessment of a program that has no relationship to the actual program. For the last study this was particularly true for the biological sciences, since the descriptive names did not match programs at their institutions. In addition to the problems with the biological sciences, there were instances at some institutions where a field may had multiple programs that were identified separately or jointly, depending on the Institutional Coordinator's interpretation of the taxonomy. There were also instances when the study field name did not fit the terminology used at the institution and a program was submitted which was inconsistent with other programs in the fields. For the next study it may be appropriate to revisit the taxonomy used in the biological sciences and in some other broad fields.

Presenters: Thomas Fox, Harvard University
                     Norman Bradburn, National Opinion Research Center

4:30 PM
F. Expanding the Focus to Industry and Government

Finding ways to factor the assessment of employment sectors outside academe into the study was of interest to the last study committee, but they did not have the time or the resources to find appropriate measures. One measure might be the identification of programs that industry or government looks to for recruiting graduates or another could be a measure industry/ university research cooperation. Another topic of interest might be an exploration of new measures that would better suit the needs of the non-academic sector.

Presenters: Stephen Lukasik, Independent Consultant

5:30 PM
Adjournment for the Day

Wednesday, June 23, 1999

8:30 AM
G. Incorporating Interdisciplinary Programs, Emerging Fields and Other Fields

The interdisciplinary sciences are playing a more and more important role in graduate education and new fields are developing that in ten years may be larger than some that are now part of the study. Finding ways to identify these programs and collect consistent information across institutions would enhance the next study. In addition, some disciplines not included in the last study, since they did not meet the degree production conditions specified by the study committee, have asked to be considered for the next study. With the understanding that interdisciplinary, emerging or smaller fields may not have the critical mass to provide valid reputational measures, is it possible to include them and still obtain meaningful evaluations.

Presenters: Debra Stewart, North Carolina State University

9:30 AM
H. Outcomes and Process of Graduate Education

One of the main deficiencies of past studies has been the inability to measure the effectiveness of graduate education. The effectiveness question on the National Survey of Graduate Faculty does not provide useful information, since very few individuals in the survey have direct knowledge of the graduate programs at a range of institutions. Finding objective measures that will provide this information is an important goal for the next study. Another aspect of graduate education, aside from the scholarship of the faculty and the outcomes of graduates, are the activities within graduate programs that can greatly enhance its quality, such as counseling, teaching instruction, and internship programs. Is it possible to measure these activities?

Presenters: Joseph Cerny, University of California, Berkeley
                John Wiley, University of Wisconsin

10:45 AM
I. Matching Measures to Program Missions

Within a given field, all research-doctoral programs do not have the same mission or educational philosophy. The purpose of some may be the education of future faculty at institutions similar to their own and others may focus their educational program on serving local industries or government facilities. The mission of programs at an institution is also tied to that of their pier institutions. Measuring dissimilar programs in a field against the same standards may not provide useful information. Can measures be found that match the mission of a program and in particular, customize reputational measures that correctly reflect the mission?

Presenters: John Vaughn, Association of American Universities
                Cora Marrett, University of Massachusetts

1:00 PM
J. Customizing Measures to Field Characteristics

Some of the measures used in past studies did not provide relevant information or sufficient information to characterize programs in specific fields. This was especially true in Arts and Humanities in the 1995 study. It is not essential that uniform measures be used across all fields. Finding the appropriate measures will be a critical element in the next study.

Agricultural and Nutritional Sciences
    Presenter: Patricia Swan, Iowa State University

Arts and Humanities
    Presenter: John D'Arms, American Council of Learned Societies

Biological Sciences
   Presenter: Robert Thach, Washington University

Engineering
   Presenter: Leonard Peters, Virginia Polytechic Institute and State University

Physical Sciences and Mathematics
   Presenter: Ronald Douglas, Texas A & M

Social and Behavioral Sciences
   Presenter: Brian Foster, University of Nebraska

3:00 PM
Adjournment

Study of Research-Doctorate Programs in the United States
Office of Scientific and Research Personnel
National Research Council

Planning Meeting

June 22-23, 1999
Washington, D.C.

PARTICIPANTS

Richard Anderson
Somat Engineering, Inc.

Marilyn Baker
National Research Council

Joseph Bordogna
National Science Foundation

Norman Bradburn
National Opinion Research Center

Joseph Cerny
University of California, Berkeley

Jonathan Cole
Columbia University

E. William Colglazier
National Research Council

Olga Collazos
Intern, National Research Council

John D'Arms
American Council of Learned Societies

Donna Dean
National Institutes of Health

Nancy Diamond
Goucher College

Ronald Douglas
Texas A&M

Brian Foster
University of Nebraska

Thomas Fox
Harvard University

Hugh Graham
Vanderbilt University

M.R.C. Greenwood
University of California, Santa Cruz

Jong-on Hahm
National Research Council

Peter Henderson
National Research Council

Stanley Ikenberry
American Council on Education

Ruth Kirschstein
National Institutes of Health

Charlotte Kuh
National Research Council

Jules LaPidus
Council of Graduate Schools

Stephen Lukaski
Independent Consultant

Lesley Lydell
University of Minnesota

Brendan Maher
Harvard University

Cora Marrett
University of Massachusetts

Lawrence Martin
State University of New York, Stony Brook

David Meyer
University of California-Los Angeles

Maresi Narad
University of California-Berkeley

Leonard Peters
Virginia Polytechnic Institute and State University

George Reinhart
National Research Council

Debra Stewart
North Carolina State University

Stephen Stigler
University of Chicago

Jennifer Sutton
National Research Council

Patricia Swan
Iowa State University

Peter Syverson
Council of Graduate Schools

Orlando Taylor
Howard University

Robert Thach
Washington University

John Vaughn
Association of American Universities

Jim Voytuk
National Research Council

Garry Walters
Ohio State Board of Regents

John Wiley
University of Wisconsin

SCHEDULE FOR COMMITTEE AND PANEL ACTIVITIES

Date	Committee/Panel	Place
April 15-16, 2002	**1st Full Committee Meeting**	Washington, D.C.
June 6-7, 2002	1st Panel on Student Processes and Outcomes Meeting	Washington, D.C.
June 17, 2002	Panel on Quantitative Measures	New York University Torch Club, NYC
June 20-21, 2002	Panel on Taxonomy and Interdisciplinarity	Washington, D.C. 5th St. Bldg
July 22, 2002	Panel on Reputational Measures and Data Presentation	Washington, D.C. 5th St. Bldg
August 1-2, 2002	**2nd Full Committee Meeting**	Woods Hole Study Center, Woods Hole, MA
September 5-6, 2002	2nd Panel on Student Processes and Outcomes meeting	Washington, D.C.
September 11-12, 2002	2nd Panel on Taxonomy & Interdisciplinarity meeting	Washington, D.C.
September 18, 2002	2nd Panel on Reputational Measures and Data Presentation meeting	Washington, D.C.
September 19, 2002	2nd Panel on the Review of Quantitative Measures meeting	New York University Torch Club, NYC
September 30-October 1, 2002	**3rd Full Committee Meeting**	Washington, D.C.
March 26-28, 2003	**4th Full Committee Meeting**	Beckman Center, Irvine, CA
July 31-August 1, 2003	**5th Full Committee Meeting**	Woods Hole Study Center, Woods Hole, MA

Committee to Examine the Methodology for the Assessment of Research Doctorate Programs

First Meeting: April 15-16, 2002
Washington, D.C.

Agenda

Monday, April 15—Green 104

9:15-9:45 AM   Bias Discussion - C. Kuh

10:00-11:00 AM   Key issues: Sponsors
                      Betsey Kuhn - United States Department of Agriculture
                      Judith Ramelly - National Science Foundation
                      Wendy Baldwin - National Institutes of Health

11:00 AM -12:00 PM   Key Issues: Conference Board of Associated Research Councils
                      Bruce Alberts - National Research Council
                      David Ward - American Council on Education

1:00-2:00 PM   Key issues: Higher Education organizations
                      Debra Stewart - Council of Graduate Schools
                      Peter McGrath - National Association of State Universities and Land-Grant Colleges
                      Nils Hasselmo - Association of American Universities

2:00-3:30 PM   Key issues: Other Interested Groups
                      Phyllis Franklin – Modern Language Association
                      Sidney Golub – Federation of American Societies for Experimental Biology
                      Frank Huband – American Society for Engineering Education
                      Robert Townsend – American Historical Association.
                      Howard Silver - Consortium of Social Science Associations

EXECUTIVE SESSION

3:45-5:00 PM   Committee discussion of key issues and study organization

Tuesday, April 16

EXECUTIVE SESSION

8:00-10:00 AM   Study Organization and NRC Report Review

10:00 AM-1:00 PM   Panel Tasks

Panel on Student Processes and Outcomes

First panel meeting: June 6-7, 2002
Washington, D.C.

Agenda

Committee Statement of Task and Charge to Student Processes and Outcomes Panel

Issues

Sample Survey Instruments

    The National Doctoral Program Survey

    Survey on Doctoral Education and Career Preparation

    Ph.D.'s Ten Years Later

    National Survey of Student Engagement

    Graduate Student Exit Questionnaires

Articles

"National Survey of Student Engagement: Conceptual Framework and Overview of Psychometric Properties" George D. Kuh

Re-envisioning the Ph.D., "What Concerns Do We Have?" Jody D. Nyquist and Bettina J. Woodford

"The National Doctoral Program Survey: Executive Summary" National Association of Graduate-Professional Students

Panel on Review of Quantitative Measures

First panel meeting: June 17, 2002
New York, NY

Agenda

Monday, June 17, 2002

9:00-9:30 AM   Introduction and Bias Discussion

9:30-10:15 AM   Faculty, Student, and Institutional Characteristics

10:45 AM-12:00 PM   Measures of Productivity

12:00-2:30 PM   Field Specific Data

2:30-3:30 PM   Data Sources and Data Collection Issues

4:00-5:00 PM   Wrap-up and Issues for Investigation

Panel on Taxonomy and Interdisciplinarity

First panel Meeting: June 20-21, 2002
Washington, DC

Agenda

Thursday, June 20, 2002

9:00-9:30 AM	Bias Discussion
9:30-10:30 AM	Study Fields Selection: Taxonomy
10:45 AM -12:00 PM	Study Fields Selection: New Fields
12:45-3:30 PM	Program Specific Issues
3:45-5:00 PM	Interdisciplinarity

Friday, June 21, 2002

8:00-9:45 AM	Small Field/Program Issues
10:00 AM -12:00 PM	Wrap-up and Items for Additional Investigation

Panel on Reputational Measures and Presentation of Data

July 22, 2002
Washington, D.C.

Agenda

9:00-10:00 AM	Introductions and bias discussion
10:00-10:45 AM	Measuring the Scholarly Reputation of Programs
11:00 AM -12:30 PM	Alternative Approaches to Measuring Reputation
12:30-1:30 PM	Working lunch: Recommendations for Pilot Testing
1:30-2:45 PM	Data Presentation
3:00-4:00 PM	Data Presentation Alternatives
4:00-5:00 PM	Recommendations to Full Committee

Committee to Examine the Methodology for the Assessment of Research Doctorate Programs

Second meeting: August 1-2, 2002
Woods Hole, Massachusetts

Agenda

August 1

CLOSED SESSION ALL DAY

8:15-8:30 AM	Minutes and Summary of Last Meeting	Ostriker
9:00-10:00 AM	Panel on Student Educational Processes and Outcomes	Lorden
10:15-11:15 AM	Panel to Review Quantitative Measures	Stimpson
11:15 AM-12:15 PM	Panel on Taxonomy and Interdisciplinarity	Solomon
1:15-2:15 PM	Panel on Reputational Measures and Data Presentation	Cole, Holland
2:15-3:15 PM	Open Issues (examples: GRE scores, report format, nonacademic constituencies)	Ostriker
3:30-5:00 PM	Outreach, participants for next meeting	Ostriker

August 2

OPEN SESSION

8:15-9:15 AM	Non-academic employers Guest: Paula Stephan, Georgia State University	Ostriker

CLOSED SESSION

9:15-10:15 AM	Pilot site strategy	Ostriker
10:30 AM-12:00 PM	Draft Report Outline	Ostriker

Panel on Student Processes and Outcomes

September 5-6, 2002
Washington, D.C.

Agenda

The entire meeting will be held in Executive Session, since its primary business is to develop recommendations for the full committee.

Thursday, September 5

9:00-9:30 AM   Minutes and Discussion of comments on panel recommendations from the full committee.

9:30-10:30 AM   Who are the audiences for this information? What do they need to know?

11:00 AM -12:00 PM   Programmatic data

                      Much of the descriptive data that the Panel has discussed has also been mentioned by the Panel on Quantitative Measures. Are there particular measures of effectiveness of the graduate program that we want to be sure is included?

1:00-2:30 PM   Rationale for surveying students

                      A. Current students
                          1. How many years past enrollment? Why?
                      B. Recent graduates
                          1. How many years past graduation? Why?
                          2. What does such a survey tell us about the current program?
                      C. Verification of program-provided information

3:00-5:00 AM   Pilot sites. What we want to learn from them.

                      Each pilot site is a different kind of institution. Do we want to customize questions according to "mission" (determined either empirically or *ex ante*). For example, do we want to ask students from programs whose graduates go predominantly to academic employment different questions from those whose graduates go primarily to industrial employment?

Friday, September 6

8:30-10:00 AM   Prioritization of respondents, questions.

                      What questions are key indicators of the quality and effectiveness of a Ph.D. program? Should they be customized by field?

10:15AM-12:00 PM   Summary of Recommendations and Rationales

Panel on Taxonomy and Interdisciplinarity

September 11-12, 2002
Washington, D.C.

Agenda

Because the entire purpose of the meeting is to draft recommendations for consideration of the full Committee, the entire meeting will be held in executive session.

Wednesday, September 11, 2002

9:00-9:30 AM   Goals of this Meeting. Summary of the Full Committee Discussion in Woods Hole

9:30-10:30 AM   Principles for Including and Excluding Programs

                        Should there be a distinction between listing a program and ranking it? Is there any reason to list programs that don't grant degrees? How can we identify them?

10:45 AM-12:00 PM   Identifying Programs in Professional Schools

                        The Panel has made the distinction between programs that primarily educate practitioners and those that primarily educate researchers. Does this distinction permit us to identify programs in professional schools that should appear in the final study? Which programs should be included (Staff will prepare a list of all Ph.D. degrees granted in professional schools.)

1:00-3:00 PM   Revisiting the Taxonomy

                        Given the morning's discussion, how comfortable is the Panel with the taxonomy it organized at its last meeting? What should be changed? What recommendations does the Panel have about treatment of faculty who teach in more than one program? Are we comfortable with how we have addressed interdisciplinarity? Do we need to address issues of multi-university centers or facilities?

3:45-4:30 PM   Structuring Pilot Site Trials

                        The pilot site trials will tell us how well the taxonomy fits each institution. If there are problems with fit, how do we design consistent rules for adjustment?

Thursday, September 12

9:00-10:00 AM   Additional Sources to Test the Taxonomy

                        The AAU has agreed to test a draft taxonomy with its chief academic officers. Are there other organizations we should ask? What kind of feedback should we request?

10:15AM-12:00 PM   Recommendations for the full committee

Panel on Reputational Measures and Presentation of Data

September 18, 2002
Washington, D.C.

Agenda

Because the entire purpose of the meeting is to draft recommendations for consideration of the full Committee, the entire meeting will be held in executive session.

Wednesday, September 18, 2002

8:30-9:00 AM	Goals of this Meeting. Minutes of the last meeting. Summary of the Full Committee Discussion in Woods Hole

9:00-10:30 AM   Possible Approaches to a Reputational Measure

At the first panel meeting there was agreement that program reputation should be measured, and that efforts should be made to better inform the raters of program characteristics. However, the procedures for conduction a reputational survey were not formulated, and some open questions are:
Who should be surveyed?
What program information should be available to the raters?
What is the format of the survey form?
What questions should be asked? Should multiple *indicators* be used to describe program quality?

11:00 AM-12:00 PM   Special Issues

In addition to the above issues, there are some special concerns, such as:
Can meaningful measures of reputation be generated for the lower half of the ratings? Should all programs be rated?
How can niche programs or programs in subfields be rated?

12:00-1:00 PM   Working Lunch: Measuring Reputation in the Non-Academic Sector

For some fields, such as those in Engineering, a large number of program graduates find employment in industry and government. Can ways be found to assess the quality of these programs from the viewpoint of their non-academic "customers"?

1:00-3:00 PM   Presentation of Reputational Data

The panel and full committee agreed that no single ordinal ranking reflects the quality of programs in a field, and other methods should be found to represent reputational data. Several methods have been proposed, including random halves, bootstrap, and a Bayesian approach. Some of these methods are illustrated in this agenda book using data fro English programs from the 1995 study. Other approaches are also described in a memo from Paul Holland, included under tab – IV. Committee Discussion.

3:15-4:00 PM   Pilot Site Trials

While testing different approaches to reputational ratings of a program is limited by the nine pilot institutions and the number of Ph.D. programs they offer, it might be possible to develop some trials that will assist in answering some procedural questions.

4:00-5:00 PM   Recommendations to the Full Committee.

Panel on Review of Quantitative Measures

September 19, 2002
New York, NY

Agenda

Because the entire purpose of the meeting is to draft recommendations for consideration of the full Committee, the entire meeting will be held in executive session.

Thursday, September 19, 2002

9:00-9:30 AM	Goals of this Meeting. Minutes of the last meeting. Summary of the Full Committee Discussion in Woods Hole
9:30-10:15 AM	Mission, Institution, and Broad Field Data

The full Committee and the Panel on Student Outcomes and Processes thought that there are some relevant data at the institutional level (e.g. endowment; student health benefits, housing, and availability of childcare; and unionization of graduate students). What data should be collected at the institutional level? At the field level (e.g. humanities, social sciences, etc.)?

10:15-11:00 AM   Programmatic Data

The Committee at its last meeting encouraged the Panel to develop a large number of program characteristics that are useful and updateable. Also, the Panel on Student Outcomes and Processes referred a number of program measures to this Panel, since they would be collected through a questionnaire for program administrators.

11:15 AM-12:00 PM   Special Issues

Measures that need special attention are:
How to measure Time-to-Degree? Completion rates?
How should data on minority students should be collected and presented?
GRE scores: the Committee recommended consideration of a mean or median measure and a measure of variability (interquartile range or variance).

12:00-1:00 PM   Working Lunch

While munching, it might be useful to think about the significance of the measures we are requesting. Are they indicators of quality? Of climate? Of affluence (or lack thereof)? How might we guide students and administrators to make sense of all these data?

1:00-3:00 PM   Measures of Faculty Characteristics

These include publications and citations, but do we want measures of faculty demographics, origins, structure? Who shall we count as faculty? How do we deal with faculty who teach or supervise dissertations in more than one program?

3:15-4:00 PM   Pilot Site Trials

Should all pilot sites be asked to answer the same questions stated the same way? Do we want to try different questions out on different sites?

4:00-5:00 PM   Recommendations to the Full Committee. Prioritization and Categorization of Measures

Committee to Examine the Methodology for the Assessment of Research-Doctorate Programs

Third Meeting: September 30-October 1, 2002
Washington, D.C.

Agenda

September 30, 2002

EXECUTIVE SESSION

8:45-9:45 AM	General Issues	Jeremiah Ostriker
	• Memo from Brendan Maher	
	• Principle	
	• Diversity	

PUBLIC SESSION

10:00-11:15 AM	Fields and Disciplines	
	• American Society for Theatre Research and Association for Theatre in Higher Education Arts	Thomas Postlewait
	• National Communication Association	Bill Balthrop
	• American Society for Microbiology	Gail Cassell
	• Association to Advance Collegiate Schools of Business	Dan LeClair

11:15 AM - 12:00 PM	Diversity in Doctoral Education	
	• Hispanic Association of Colleges and Universities	Gumecindo Salas
	• Council of Historically Black Graduate Schools	Irene Johnson
	• National Black Graduate Student Association	Theodore Bunch, Jr.

EXECUTIVE SESSION

12:30 – 1:30 PM	Report of the Panel on Taxonomy and Interdisciplinarity	Walter Cohen, *Panel Co-chair* Frank Solomon, *Panel Co-chair*
1:30-2:30 PM	Report of the Panel on Student Processes and Outcomes	Joan Lorden, *Panel Chair*
2:30-3:30 PM	Report of the Panel on Quantitative Measures	Catharine Stimpson, *Panel Chair*
3:30-4:30 PM	Report of Panel on Reputational Measures and Data Presentation	Jonathan Cole, *Panel Co-chair* Paul Holland, *Panel Co-chair*

Tuesday, October 1, 2002

EXECUTIVE SESSION

8:30-10:00 AM	Pilot Site Strategy
10:15-10:45 AM	Outreach
10:45 AM - 12:00 PM	Further discussion of issues arising from the Panel reports

Committee to Examine the Methodology for the Assessment of Research-Doctorate Programs

March 26-28, 2003
Irvine, California

Agenda

The entire meeting will be held in Executive Session

Wednesday, March 26, 2003, Newport Room

2:10 - 2:20PM   Minutes of Sept. 30- Oct. 1, 2002, Meeting

2:20 – 2:45 PM   Bias Discussion

2:45 – 5:00 PM   Findings from the Pilot Trials   Charlotte Kuh, Jim Voytuk

Thursday, March 27, 2003

8:15 – 10:30 AM   Discussion of Preliminary Findings and Recommendations

10:45 AM– 12:00 PM   Writing Groups:
                    1. Student Outcomes/Quantitative Measures   Newport Room
                    2. Reputational Measures   Crystal Cove Room
                    3. Taxonomy   Laguna Room
                    4. Extra Breakout Room   Emerald Bay Room

1:00 – 5:00 PM   Writing Groups: Breakout Room

Friday, March 28, 2003

8:15 – 11:30 AM   Reconvene in the Newport Room
                    • Discussion of report text
                    • Remaining tasks
                    • Next steps

Assessment of Research-Doctorate Programs
J. Erik Jonnson Woods Hole Study Center

July 31 – August 1, 2003, Meeting

Agenda

Thursday, July 31, 2003

8:45 AM	Minutes of March 26-27, 2003, Meeting
9:00 AM	NRC Review Process—Next Steps
9:30 AM	Discussion on "Response to Report Review" Chapter-by-Chapter

Friday, August 1, 2003

8:30 AM   Findings since the Last Meeting
a. Relating Qualitative to Quantitative Measures
b. Student Questionnaires
c. Outside Raters
  • Fields for Outside Raters
  • What Kind of People Are We Looking for?

10:00 AM   The Next Committee
  • Proposal—Major Points
  • Possible Committee Members

12:00 PM   Adjourn.

Appendix D

Sample Questionnaires

(These questionnaires are subject to further review and revision.)

1. Institutional Questionnaire

2. Program Questionnaire

3. Faculty Questionnaire

4. Student Questionnaires

   a. Questionnaire for Admitted-to-Candidacy Doctoral Students

   b. Questionnaire for Program Graduates

Institutional Questionnaire

To the institutional coordinator: This questionnaire is intended to collect data about university-provided resources that are available to all doctoral programs. Typically, the ideal respondent will be in the university's office of institutional research. Most of the questions apply to all programs. One, on laboratory space, applies only to the sciences (including some social sciences). In listing programs, please refer to the attached taxonomy and answer for those programs that are present at your institution.

1. For the libraries at your institution: (Please enter the average over the past three years)

    a. What is the average size of your professional library staff in total FTEs? _____
    b. What is the average annual library budget? _____
    c. What is the average annual budget for acquisition of books? _____
    d. What is the average annual budget for acquisition of:
         print journals _____   electronic journals_____ ?
    e. What is the average annual budget for microprint and electronic databases? _____

2. Is health care insurance available to graduate students under an institutional plan?
                    Yes   No
    a. If available, health care insurance is made available to:
                    ☐ Students only   ☐ Students and faculty

    b. If available, what is the level of institutional support? (Check all that apply)

            Institution covers premium costs for:
            ☐ Teaching assistants ☐ Research assistants
            ☐ All other full-time graduate students ☐ All graduate students

            Institution covers partial premium costs for:
            ☐ Teaching assistants ☐ Research assistants
            ☐ All other full-time graduate students ☐ All graduate students

            No institutional contribution for:
            ☐ Teaching assistants ☐ Research assistants ☐ Other graduate students

3. Does the university provide childcare facilities that are available to graduate students?
                    ☐ Yes ☐ No

    a. If yes, is the cost subsidized by the institution?
                    ☐ Yes ☐ No

    b. If not, does the institution provide a listing of childcare providers to graduate students?
                    ☐ Yes ☐ No

4. Is university-subsidized student housing available to doctoral students?
                    ☐ Yes ☐ No

If so, what is the percentage of the doctoral students who live in university-provided housing? _____

5. Are graduate students are unionized on your campus?

☐ Yes ☐ No

If yes, ☐ Some students ☐ All students

If yes, are teaching assistants unionized? ☐ Yes ☐ No
    If yes, ☐ Some teaching assistants ☐ All teaching assistants

If yes, are research assistants unionized? ☐ Yes ☐ No
    If yes, ☐ Some research assistants ☐ All research assistants?

6. Which of the following apply to the doctoral program at the institutional level?

    a. The institution confers awards to honor graduate students for teaching and/or research.
       ☐ Yes ☐ No

    b. Awards are given to faculty for mentoring or other activities that promote scholarship of doctoral students.
       ☐ Yes ☐ No

    c. The institution provides some form of travel support for doctoral students to attend professional meetings.
       ☐ Yes ☐ No

    d. There is an organized program at the institutional level to help doctoral students improve their teaching skills.
       ☐ Yes ☐ No

    e. The institution provides an office that assists doctoral students in learning about employment opportunities. ☐ Yes ☐ No

7. **For the information displayed in the following table, please provide in a file sent by email to rdpilot@nas.edu**
For the each doctoral program in science (including the social sciences) and engineering at your institution, what is the net assignable square feet (NASF) of research space dedicated to the program (exclude space that is used only for undergraduates)? Please use the same definitions for NASF and research space that are used in the NSF Survey of Scientific and Engineering Research Facilities. See [Taxonomy] for a list of the program fields in the study, and provide the information in the Email file for only those doctoral programs that are offered at your institution.

Program	Research space NASF	Shared space with other programs (Y/N)
Program #1		
Program #2		
Program #3		

Program Questionnaire

Background Information

This information will enable the National Research Council to contact you if there are any questions about the data. It will also permit us to contact faculty for the purpose of administering a questionnaire to elicit reputational ratings and background data and to contact students to obtain information about their perceptions of the practices and offerings of the doctoral program.

Please note that in addition to the web questionnaire, we would like lists of faculty and previous employers to be sent to us via e-mail.

Please indicate the doctoral program to which the following information applies

_____

1. Please provide the name and e-mail address of the program respondent who will serve as the primary contact with the graduate program.
   Name: _____
   Title: _____
   E-mail address: _____
   Mailing Address: _____

   _____
   City_____State_____Zip Code_____

   If this is an interdisciplinary program, please list the departments affiliated with the program.

   _____

   _____

For each individual identified in questions 2 and 3, please provide in a file sent by email to rdpilot@nas.edu the information displayed in the table for the question.

2. Program Faculty: For each faculty member or senior research fellow or associate who participates in your doctoral program by directing theses, serving on doctoral committees, or teaching graduate courses, please provide the following information.

Name	Rank	Highest Degree	Gender (M or F)	Race/ Ethnicity	US Citizen or Permanent Resident (Y/N)	Tenure Status	E-mail Address

3. Faculty Employment History: For each faculty member listed in Question 2 who joined your program within the past five years, please provide the institution, company, or organization where he or she was employed immediately before joining your institution.

Name	Prior employer	Position at that employer

4. For the doctoral students in your program, please provide the number of students that fall into each of the following categories.

    a.   Total number of students: _____

    b.   Status: Full-time _____ Part-time _____ Unknown _____

    c.   Gender: Male _____ Female _____Unknown _____

    d.   Citizenship: U.S. _____
                             Permanent Resident _____
                             Temporary Visa _____
                             Unknown _____

    d.   Race/Ethnicity (if U.S. citizen or Permanent Residents)

                    American Indian or Alaskan Native _____
                    Asian or Pacific Islander _____
                    Black _____
                    White _____
                    Hispanic _____
                          Mexican American _____
                          Puerto Rican _____
                          Other _____
                    Multiracial _____
                    Unknown _____

    e.   Percentage of doctoral students with master's degree _____

Program Information

5. Does your program have a mission statement?

                           ☐ Yes   ☐ No

    If so, what is the mission statement? (50 words or less)

    _____
    _____
    _____
    _____

    If there are particular areas of research emphasis in your doctoral program, please choose from the subfields in [Taxonomy]:

    _____   _____
    _____   _____

_____   _____
_____   _____
_____   _____

6. How many Ph.D.s have been awarded in the program in each of the past five years? (Note: Years span from July 1 to June 30)

    2001-02 _____   2000-01 _____   1999-00 _____   1998-99 _____   1997-98 _____

7. For each of the academic years listed in the following table, enter the number of students who entered the program in the year and the number who completed their degrees in 4, 6, or 8, years or are still in the program. (Note: Years span from July 1 to June 30)

Entering Student Academic Year Cohort	Number of Entering Doctoral Students	Number of Students admitted to candidacy by the end of the 4th year of enrollment	Of those admitted to candidacy, number who complete within 4 years	Of those admitted to candidacy, number who complete within 6 years	Of those admitted to candidacy, number who complete within 8 years	Of those admitted to candidacy, how many are still enrolled after 8 years?
1992-1993						
1993-1994						
1994-1995						
1995-1996						
1996-1997						
1997-1998						
1998-1999						
1999-2000						
2000-2001						
2001-2002						

7a. Averaged over the past three years, what percent of entering students withdrew from the program before completing two years of study? _____%

7b. Averaged over the past three years, what has been the median time to degree for those who completed the program? _____ (Note: the median time is the number of years it takes half of the number of students from the same entering year who are admitted to candidacy to complete their degree.)

8. Is a master's degree required of students prior to admission to your program?
                         ☐ Yes   ☐ No

9. What proportion of your full-time first-year doctoral students receive full support throughout their first year (tuition and an adequate living allowance provided as stipend or salary in program related work (TA or RA)? _____

10. How many years of full financial support could students entering your doctoral program expect to receive from your institution or an external source? _____

11. Over the past five years approximately what fraction of the first-year students in your program received financial support either from your institution or from extramural grants or fellowships?

                    Tuition only _____
                    Tuition and stipend_____
                    Stipend only_____

12. What proportion of currently enrolled doctoral students in your program (included in multiple categories if appropriate) are currently supported by:

                    Externally funded fellowships: _____
                    Externally funded traineeships: _____
                    Externally funded research assistantships: _____
                    University funded teaching assistantships: _____
                    University funded research assistantships: _____
                    University funded tuition waivers, fellowships, or stipends: _____

13. Averaged over the past three years, what are the average and minimum GRE scores for students accepted into the program?

      Average Verbal GRE: _____   Average Quantitative GRE: ___
      Minimum Verbal GRE: _____   Minimum Quantitative GRE: __
      Do you require GRE subject scores for all students entering the program?
                              ☐ Yes ☐ No

14. In each of the last three academic years, how many students did you accept into your doctoral program, and how many enrolled?

	Accepted	Enrolled
2000-2001	_____	_____
2001-2002	_____	_____
2002-2003	_____	_____

15. What percentage of the doctoral students in your program have individually assigned workspaces for their exclusive use?

            TAs   _____ RAs _____ All students _____

16. On average, how many courses per term is each graduate teaching assistant in the program expected to teach or assist a faculty member in teaching?

      With sole responsibility _____ As an Assistant to a faculty member _____

17. Which of the following apply to your doctoral program?

a. The program confers awards to honor graduate students for teaching and/or research.

☐ Yes ☐ No

b. Awards are given to faculty for mentoring or other activities that promote scholarship of doctoral students.

☐ Yes ☐ No

c. The program provides some form of travel support for doctoral students to attend professional meetings.

☐ Yes ☐ No

d. There is an organized program to help doctoral students improve their teaching skills.

☐ Yes ☐ No

e. The program provides organized assistance to help doctoral students explore employment opportunities.

☐ Yes ☐ No

18. List up to 5 institutions with which your program normally competes for graduate students:

Institution #1_____

Institution #2_____

Institution #3_____

Institution #4_____

Institution #5_____

19. Does your program collect data about employment outcomes for your graduates?

☐ Yes ☐ No

If yes, do you provide potential applicants with this information?

☐ Yes ☐ No

20. Please list those interdisciplinary centers in which doctoral students from your program participate (conduct research or teach).

_____

_____

_____

_____

Faculty Questionnaire

This questionnaire is part of the National Research Council's Pilot Test of the Assessment of Research Doctoral Programs. Your university has volunteered to participate in this pilot test to assist the National Research Council's study of the methodology used to assess doctoral programs. Further information about the methodology study may be found at www7.nationalacademies.org/resdoc/index.html

You have been selected to receive this questionnaire because you are a member of the faculty who participates in the education of doctoral students at your university. This means that you either teach courses to doctoral students or supervise their dissertations. If this is not the case, please indicate that in question 1.

The assessment of research doctoral programs is conducted approximately every ten years and consists of a reputational survey of doctoral programs and the collection of data about doctoral faculty and students in fifty-seven areas of study. This questionnaire provides information that will assist the study in a number of ways: 1)it will help us construct a pool from which to select raters for the reputational survey; 2)it will provide us enough information about you that we can collect data on grants, citations, and publications from other sources; and 3)it will permit a statistical description of the faculty in the graduate program or programs with which you are affiliated. Your answers will be treated as completely confidential by the National Research Council and will only be released as part of a statistical analysis.

I.   Program Identification

   a.   Do you supervise dissertations, serve on doctoral committees, or teach graduate courses in a doctoral program?

   ☐   Yes   ☐   No

   If your answer was "No", you do not need to complete the rest of the questionnaire.

   b.   From the pulldown list, please choose the program of your primary affiliation/appointment

   _____[Pull Down List of Res-Doc Programs]
   If you have difficulty locating your program on the list, please refer to the [Taxonomy] list with fields and subfields

   c.   Please list all programs in which you supervise dissertations, serve on dissertation committees, or teach graduate courses and the average percentage of your time during the past year that you spent in all activities for each program with which you are associated. (Do not list programs where you are an outside reader.)

Program	Supervise dissertations (Y/N)	Teach courses (Y/N)	Serve on dissertation committees (Y/N)	Percent of time spent in all activities for this program (total = 100%)

   d.   For the articles and books that you have published in the past five years, please list what fields you have published in Table 1. If you have a single publication that spans multiple fields, please indicate them and their fields in Table 2.

Table 1: Books and articles in a single field published in the past 3 years

Field (see Taxonomy)	Articles	Books

Table 2: Books and articles in multiple fields published in the past 3 years

Field (Enter all that apply)	Articles	Books

II. Current Employment

a. Department affiliation: _____

b. Rank: ☐ Instructor ☐ Assistant Professor
☐ Associate Professor ☐ Full Professor ☐ Other _____

c. Tenure status: ☐ Tenure-track, not tenured
☐ Tenured
☐ Non-tenure-track

d. Year first employed at current institution: [If employment was not continuous, please list year of most recent appointment at this institution.] _____

e. Have you received an extramural grant or contract support in the past year?
☐ Yes ☐ No

f. Subfields of current research interest (refer to [Taxonomy] with subfields):
Subfield # 1: _____
Subfield #2: _____
Subfield #3: _____

g. Do you consider part of your research to be interdisciplinary? ☐ Yes ☐ No
If so, what is the area of that research? _____

h. Under what names or variants of your name have you published books or articles?
_____

III. Prior Experience

What was your status prior to your current position?
☐ Student ☐ Postdoc ☐ Faculty. ☐ Other: _____

Previous employer: _____
Address: _____

City_____State/Country_____Zip Code_____
Title: _____
Employment Sector:
☐ Industry (for profit)
☐ National laboratory
☐ State or local government
☐ Federal government agency
☐ International agency
☐ 4-year college or university
☐ 2-year college
☐ K-12 school
☐ Hospital or clinic
☐ Foundation or nonprofit
☐ Military
☐ Other (specify: _____)

IV. Educational Background

a. Highest degree earned: ☐ Bachelor's ☐ Master's ☐ Ph.D.
    ☐ Professional (M.D., J.D., D.V.M., for example)

b. Institution that conferred highest degree:

    _____

c. Field of highest degree:

    _____[Pulldown List]
    Other: _____

d. Year of highest degree: _____

e. To what extent does the field of your current research, teaching, or professional activities differ
    from the field of your highest degree?
    ☐ Very similar   ☐ Somewhat similar   ☐ Very different

V. Demographic Information

a. Date of birth: _____(mm/dd/yy)

b. Gender: ☐ Male
                ☐ Female

c. Citizenship ☐ U.S.
                 ☐ Permanent Resident
                 ☐ Temporary Visa

d. Race/Ethnicity (if U.S. citizen or permanent resident)
                 ☐ American Indian or Alaskan Native
                 ☐ Asian or Pacific Islander
                 ☐ Black
                 ☐ White

☐ Hispanic (☐ Mexican American, ☐ Puerto Rican, ☐ Other)
☐ Multiracial

VI. Please provide your preferred e-mail address (where you can be reached if there are questions.)

_____

Thank you for your time.

Questionnaire for Admitted-to-Candidacy Doctoral Students

This questionnaire is part of the National Research Council's Pilot Test of the Assessment of Research Doctoral Programs. Your university has volunteered to participate in this pilot test to assist the National Research Council's study of the methodology used to assess doctoral programs. One innovation we are considering is adding student responses about the educational processes of the program. We believe that students' input is important to improving the quality of the educational experience. Further information about the methodology study may be found at www7.nationalacademies.org/resdoc/index.html

You have been selected to receive this questionnaire because you are a student who has completed over half of your doctoral program. If this is not the case, please indicate that in question 1.

The assessment of research doctoral programs is conducted approximately every ten years and consists of a reputational survey of doctoral programs and the collection of data about doctoral faculty and students in fifty-four areas of study. This questionnaire will provide information that will assist the study in a number of ways: 1) it will provide a statistical description of students in your program; 2) it will provide information about practices in your program; and 3) it will help future students in the selection of graduate programs.

Your answers will be treated as completely confidential by the National Research Council and will only be released as part of a statistical analysis. Individual answers will not be shared with faculty or administrators of your doctoral program except in aggregated form.

Institution: _____

Doctoral Program: _____

1. Educational Program

    A. Year of enrollment in this doctoral program: _____

    B. Year you expect to receive your doctorate: _____

    C. Did you (or will you) receive a master's degree before this doctorate? ☐ Yes ☐ No

    D. Did you (or will you) receive a master's degree in your doctoral field as part of your training?
        ☐ Yes ☐ No

        If yes, did you write a master's thesis? ☐ Yes ☐ No

    E. During the course of your study for the Ph.D. will you also receive any of the following as part of a joint, concurrent, or combined degree program:
        Professional doctorate (e.g., MD, DDS, OD, JD)? ☐ Yes ☐ No
        Professional master's (e.g., MBA, MPA, MPH)? ☐ Yes ☐ No

    F. During the course of your study for the Ph.D. will you also receive a certificate in another field?
        ☐ Yes ☐ No

G. What were your career goals at the time you entered graduate school? [check all that apply]
   U.S. Employment:
   ☐ Industry ☐ Government ☐ Nonprofit ☐ University
   ☐ 2-yr. college ☐ 4-yr. college Other: _____

   Non-U.S. Employment:
   ☐ Industry ☐ Government ☐ Nonprofit ☐ University
   ☐ 2-yr. college ☐ 4-yr. college Other: _____
   ☐ Unknown

H. What are your current career plans? [check all that apply]
   U.S. Employment:
   ☐ Industry ☐ Government ☐ Nonprofit ☐ University
   ☐ 2-yr. college ☐ 4-yr. college Other: _____

   Non-U.S. Employment:
   ☐ Industry ☐ Government ☐ Nonprofit ☐ University
   ☐ 2-yr. college ☐ 4-yr. college Other: _____
   ☐ Unknown

I. Of the following sources of support, which have been your primary sources during your doctoral studies? (Check the three largest)
   1. ☐ Personal/family funds
   2. ☐ Research Assistant (RA)
   3. ☐ Teaching Assistant (TA)
   4. ☐ Training grant
   5. ☐ Fellowship
   6. ☐ Loans
   7. ☐ Concurrent employment related to your degree
   8. ☐ Concurrent employment unrelated to your degree

2. Program Characteristics

A. Professional Development

   1. During your doctoral program have you received (or will you receive) instruction, practice or professional development training in:
      a. Oral communication and presentation skills: ☐ Yes ☐ No
      b. Writing proposals for funding: ☐ Yes ☐ No
      c. Preparing articles for publication: ☐ Yes ☐ No
      d. Working in collaborative groups: ☐ Yes ☐ No
      e. Conducting independent research/scholarship: ☐ Yes ☐ No
      f. Project management ☐ Yes ☐ No
      g. Research / professional ethics ☐ Yes ☐ No
      h. Speaking to nonacademic audiences ☐ Yes ☐ No

2. In your doctoral program did you have an opportunity to obtain teaching experience?
    Check the type(s) of teaching experience you have had:
    - a.   mentoring a high school student   ☐
    - b.   mentoring an undergraduate student   ☐
    - c.   grading papers for undergraduate or graduate courses   ☐
    - d.   leading discussion sections of undergraduate or graduate courses   ☐
    - e.   leading laboratory sections of undergraduate or graduate courses   ☐
    - f.   lecturing in undergraduate or graduate courses   ☐
    - g.   tutoring undergraduates   ☐

If you have had teaching experience, please answer the following,
    - h. I received formal instruction in teaching.   ☐ Yes   ☐ No
    - i. I received formal supervision and evaluation.   ☐ Yes   ☐ No
    - j. I had opportunities to teach in a variety of academic environments.
                                                              ☐ Yes   ☐ No

B. Program Environment

    1.   Does your program provide an annual or more frequent assessment of your progress?
                                                    ☐ Yes   ☐ No
    2.   Do you receive timely feedback on your research?
                                                    ☐ Yes   ☐ No
    3.   Do you have access to career advice covering a variety of employment sectors?
                                                    ☐ Yes   ☐ No
         a. If yes, are you encouraged to use it?   ☐ Yes   ☐ No

    4.   Do you have one or more faculty members at your institution that you consider
         mentors (i.e., individuals from whom you seek advice about your education, career
         development, and other matters of concern to you as a graduate student)?
             ☐ Yes   ☐ No

    5.   How would you rate the quality of teaching by faculty in your program?
                    ☐ Excellent   ☐ Good   ☐ Fair   ☐ Poor
    6.   How would you rate the quality of your research experience?
                    ☐ Excellent   ☐ Good   ☐ Fair   ☐ Poor
    7.   How would you rate the curriculum of your Ph.D. program?
                    ☐ Excellent   ☐ Good   ☐ Fair   ☐ Poor
    8.   How would you rate the overall quality of your program?
                    ☐ Excellent   ☐ Good   ☐ Fair   ☐ Poor
    9.   How would you rate the intellectual liveliness of your program?
                    ☐ Excellent   ☐ Good   ☐ Fair   ☐ Poor
    10. Considering the overall intellectual environment of your university, how much do you
         feel you have benefited from it?
                    ☐ A lot   ☐ Some   ☐ A little   ☐ Not at all

C. Infrastructure
    1. Does your program give you access to:
        a. Your own personal work space   ☐ Yes   ☐ No
        b. Computer facilities   ☐ Yes   ☐ No
        c. Other research facilities; if so, describe: _____
    2. Does your program provide adequate space for interaction among students?
                              ☐ Yes   ☐ No

    3. Are the library resources available to you adequate to support your research and
       education?   ☐ Yes   ☐ No

D. Research productivity
    1. How many research presentations (including poster presentations) have you made at
       research conferences
             a. on your campus?   _____
             b. at national or regional meetings?   _____
    2. How many research publications have you authored or co-authored during your
       doctoral studies (include pieces accepted for publication but not yet published)?
             a. Refereed articles   _____
             b. Book chapters   _____
             c. Reviews   _____
             d. Books or edited volumes   _____

3. Background Information

    A. Date of birth: _____(mm/dd/yy)

    B. Gender: ☐ Male
                   ☐ Female

    C. Citizenship   ☐ U.S.
                   ☐ Permanent Resident
                   ☐ Temporary Visa

    D. Race/Ethnicity (if U.S. citizen)
                   ☐ American Indian or Alaskan Native
                   ☐ Asian or Pacific Islander
                   ☐ Black
                   ☐ White
                   ☐ Hispanic (☐ Mexican American, ☐ Puerto Rican, ☐ Other)
                   ☐ Multiracial

    E. Dependent care responsibilities:
      1. Number of children living with you:
            Age 6 or under _____   Over age 6 _____

      3. Parents or other dependents
            ☐ Yes   ☐ No

G. Marital Status:
    Do you have a spouse or partner who lives with you?
        ☐ Yes   ☐ No

F. Level of Parents' Education: Mother   Father

        High school diploma or less   ☐   ☐
        Some college/Bachelor's degree   ☐   ☐
        Advanced degree   ☐   ☐

Five–Seven Years Post-Ph.D Questionnaire

This questionnaire is part of the National Research Council's Pilot Test of the Assessment of Research Doctoral Programs. Your university has volunteered to participate in this pilot test to assist the National Research Council's study of the methodology used to assess doctoral programs. One innovation that we are considering is to add student responses to questions about the educational process of the program. Further information about the methodology study may be found at www7.nationalacademies.org/resdoc/index.html

You have been selected to receive this questionnaire because you are a student who has received a Ph.D. from this program five to seven years ago. If this is not the case, please indicate that in question 1.

The assessment of research doctoral programs is conducted approximately every ten years and consists of a reputational survey of doctoral programs and the collection of data about doctoral faculty and students in fifty-four areas of study. This questionnaire provides information that will assist the study in a number of ways: 1) it will help us learn whether a high enough percentage of students respond so that we can add student observations to the larger study; 2) it will provide us enough information about practices in your program that we can compare the practices of graduate programs in your field at different universities; and 3) it will permit a statistical description of the first-year students in the graduate program. Your answers will be treated as completely confidential by the National Research Council and will only be released as part of a statistical analysis. Individual answers will not be shared with faculty or administrators of your former doctoral program except in aggregated form.

1. Educational Program

   a. Name of the program where you received your Ph.D. degree:

   _____

   b. Year of enrollment in the above Ph.D. program: _____

   c. Year you received your Ph.D.: _____

   d. Did you receive a master's degree at this institution before this Ph.D.? ☐ Yes ☐ No

   e. Were you enrolled as a full-time student throughout your Ph.D. program?
      ☐ Yes ☐ No

   f. Did you attend graduate school prior to enrollment in the above Ph.D. program?
      ☐ Yes ☐ No

      If so, what degrees or certificates, if any, do you hold?
      ☐ Certificate ☐ Master's ☐ Doctoral ☐ Professional

   g. What was your career goal when you completed your Ph.D.?
      U.S. Employment:
      ☐ Industry ☐ Government ☐ Nonprofit ☐ University
      ☐ 2-yr. college ☐ 4-yr. college Other: _____

Non-U.S. Employment:
☐ Industry ☐ Government ☐ Nonprofit ☐ University
☐ 2-yr. college ☐ 4-yr. college Other: _____

☐ Unknown

h. Have your career goals changed since you received your Ph.D.?
☐ Yes   ☐ No

i. During your Ph.D. program, were you supported by funds from outside the institution?
☐ Yes   ☐ No
(Check all that apply)
Type: ☐ Fellowship ☐ Training Grant ☐ Research Grant
☐ Your employer ☐ Other(Specify:_____)

j. Did you receive institutional support?
☐ Yes   ☐ No
(Check all that apply)
Type: ☐ Teaching Assistantship ☐ Research Assistantship ☐ Fellowship
☐ Tuition scholarship or waiver only ☐ Loan ☐ None ☐ Other(Specify:_)

2. **Employment and Career Status**

a. First employer or place of postdoctoral study after Ph.D. completion:
Name: _____
Address: _____
City_____State/Country_____Zip Code_____
Title: _____

b. Employment Sector:
☐ Industry (for profit)
☐ National laboratory
☐ State or local government
☐ Federal government agency
☐ International agency
☐ University
☐ 4-year college
☐ 2-year college
☐ K-12 school
☐ Hospital or clinic
☐ Foundation or nonprofit
☐ Military
☐ Other (specify)

c. If you hold or have held a postdoctoral position or positions, how many _____, and at what institutions, companies or government agencies were they located? List chronologically starting with the most recent.

Position # 1: _____   Dates: _____
Position # 2: _____   Dates: _____
Position # 3: _____   Dates: _____
Position # 4: _____   Dates: _____

d. Current employer:

Name: _____

Address: _____

City_____State/Country_____Zip Code_____

Title: _____

e. Current Employment Sector:

☐ Industry (for profit)
☐ National laboratory
☐ State or local government
☐ Federal government agency
☐ International agency
☐ University
☐ 4-year college
☐ 2-year college
☐ K-12 school
☐ Hospital or clinic
☐ Foundation or nonprofit
☐ Military
☐ Other (specify)

3. Ph.D. Program Characteristics

a. During your Ph.D. education, in which of the following areas was training PROVIDED, which skills or experiences have you USED since graduation, and which area do you wish you had learned MORE about? (check all that apply)

1) Teaching experiemce   ☐ Provided ☐ Used ☐ More

2) Oral communication; presentation skills
                                 ☐ Provided ☐ Used ☐ More

3) Writing proposals for funding   ☐ Provided ☐ Used ☐ More

4) Manuscript preparation   ☐ Provided ☐ Used ☐ More

5) Experience working in collaborative groups
                                 ☐ Provided ☐ Used ☐ More

6) Critical analysis   ☐ Provided ☐ Used ☐ More

7) Locating and applying information   ☐ Provided ☐ Used ☐ More

8) Experience working with people of varied educational levels
☐ Provided ☐ Used ☐ More

9) Experience working with people from diverse backgrounds
☐ Provided ☐ Used ☐ More

10) Experience working in teams ☐ Provided ☐ Used ☐ More

b. Research Productivity

1) How many books or edited books have you published or are currently accepted for publication? __

2) How many articles or book chapters have you published or are currently accepted for publication? __

3) How many books or articles have you reviewed for publication? _____

4) How many reviews, enumerated in 3), have been or will be published? ___

5) How many refereed papers have you or a coauthor presented at professional conferences? _____

6) How many awards have you received? (Respond to all categories.)
a) For teaching: _____
b) For research: _____
c) From professional societies: _____
d) From your institution or employer:_____

7) How many patents or licenses have you received? _____

8) How many grants have you received from your employer or institution? ____

9) How many grants have you received from extramural funding agencies? ___

4. Background Information

a. Date of birth: _____(mm/dd/yy)

b. Gender: ☐ Male
              ☐ Female

c. Citizenship ☐ U.S.
                ☐ Permanent Resident
                ☐ Temporary Visa

d. Race/Ethnicity (if U.S. citizen)
- ☐ American Indian or Alaskan Native
- ☐ Asian
- ☐ Pacific Islander
- ☐ Black
- ☐ White
- ☐ Hispanic (☐ Mexican American, ☐ Puerto Rican, ☐ Other)
- ☐ Multiracial

e. Martial Status ☐ Married
                 ☐ Single

f. Number of Children: Age 6 and under _____ Over age 6 _____

g. Level of Parents' Education:

	Mother	Father
Less than high school	☐	☐
High school diploma	☐	☐
Some college	☐	☐
Bachelor's degree	☐	☐
Master's degree	☐	☐
Professional degree	☐	☐
Doctoral degree	☐	☐

h. Is English your first language? ☐ Yes ☐ No

Appendix E

Taxonomy of Fields and Their Subfields

LIFE SCIENCES

Biochemistry, Biophysics, and Structural Biology
  Biochemistry
  Biophysics
  Structural Biology
Cell Biology
Developmental Biology
Ecology and Evolutionary Biology
  Behavior and Ethology
  Biogeochemistry
  Evolution
  Population Biology
  Physiological Ecology
  Terrestrial and Aquatic Ecology
Genetics, Genomics, and Bioinformatics
  Bioinformatics
  Genetics
  Genomics
Immunology and Infectious Disease
  Immunity
  Immunology of Infectious Disease
  Immunopathology
  Immunoprophylaxis and Therapy
  Parasitology
Microbiology
  Environmental Microbiology and Ecology
  Microbial Physiology
  Pathogenic Microbiology
  Virology
Molecular Biology
Neuroscience and Neurobiology
  Cognitive Neuroscience
  Computational Neuroscience
  Molecular and Cellular Neuroscience
  Systems Neuroscience

Pharmacology, Toxicology, and Environmental Health
  Environmental Health
  Pharmacology
  Toxicology
  Medicinal/Pharmaceutical Chemistry
Physiology
Animal Sciences
  Aquaculture and Fisheries
  Domestic Animal Sciences
  Wildlife Science
Entomology
Food Science and Engineering
  Food Engineering and Processing
  Food Microbiology
  Food Chemistry
  Food Biotechnology
Nutrition
  Animal
  Human, Community, and International
Plant Sciences
  Agronomy and Crop Sciences
  Forestry and Forest Sciences
  Horticulture
  Plant Pathology
  Plant Breeding and Genetics
Emerging Fields:
  Biotechnology
  Systems Biology

PHYSICAL SCIENCES, MATHEMATICS AND ENGINEERING

Applied Mathematics
Astrophysics and Astronomy
Chemistry

Computer Science
  Artificial Intelligence
  Programming Languages
  Systems
  Theory
Earth Sciences
  Environmental Sciences
  Geology
  Geochemistry
  Geophysics and Seismology
  Paleontology
  Soil Science
Mathematics
  Algebra, Number Theory, and Algebraic Geometry
  Analysis
  Discrete Mathematics and Combinatorics
  Geometry
  Logic
  Topology
Oceanography, Atmospheric Sciences, and Meteorology
  Atmospheric Sciences
  Fresh Water Studies
  Meteorology
  Oceanography
Physics
  Atomic, Molecular, and Optical Physics
  Condensed Matter Physics
  Cosmology, Relativity, and Gravity
  Elementary Particles, Fields, and String Theory
  Engineering Physics
  Fluids
  Nuclear
  Plasma
  Quantum
Statistics and Probability
  Biostatistics
  Probability
  Statistical Theory
Aerospace Engineering
Biological and Agricultural Engineering
  Agricultural Engineering, including Microbial Systems
  Bioinstrumentation and Measurement including
    Microscopy and Imaging
Biomedical Engineering
  Biomechanics
  Biomolecular Engineering, including Cell and Tissue
    Engineering
Chemical Engineering
Civil and Environmental Engineering
  Environmental Engineering
  Environmental Fluid Mechanics and Hydrology
  Environmental Systems Engineering
  Geotechnical Engineering
  Remote Sensing
  Structural Engineering

Transportation Systems Engineering
  Water Resource Systems
Electrical and Computer Engineering
  Computer Engineering
  Communications Engineering
  Electrical and Electronics
Materials Science and Engineering
  Biology and Bio-Inspired Materials
  Environmental Materials
  Functional and Device Materials
  Structural
Mechanical Engineering
Operations Research, Systems Engineering, and Industrial
    Engineering
  Industrial Engineering
  Operational Research
  Systems Engineering
Emerging Field:
  Information Science
  Nanoscience and Nanotechnology

SOCIAL AND BEHAVIORAL SCIENCES

Agricultural and Resource Economics
Anthropology
  Archaeological
  Biological and Physical
  Social and Cultural
Communication
  Communication Studies
  Mass Communication
  Speech and Rhetorical Studies
Economics
  Behavioral Economics
  Econometrics
  Economic Theory
  Growth and Development
  Industrial Organization
  International Economics
  Labor Economics
  Public Economics
Geography and Regional Science
Linguistics
  Applied (includes Second Language Acquisition)
  Comparative and Historical Linguistics, and Linguistic
    Diversity
  Computational
  Psycholinguistics
  Sociolinguistics
  Semantics, Syntax, and Phonology
Political Science
  American Politics
  Comparative Politics
  International Relations
  Models and Methods

Political Theory
Public Policy
Psychology
   Biological Psychology
   Clinical and Abnormal Psychology
   Cognitive Psychology
   Developmental Psychology
   Industrial and Organizational Psychology
   Social Psychology
Sociology
   Criminology
   Historical Sociology
   Methods and Mathematical Sociology
   Social Stratification, including Race and Ethnicity
   Theory
Emerging Field:
   Organizations, Occupations, and Work
   Science and Technology Studies

ARTS AND HUMANITIES

American Studies
Classics
   Classical Literature and Philology
   Ancient History (Greek and Roman through Late
      Antiquity)
   Ancient Philosophy
   Classical Archaeology and Art History
   Indo-European Linguistics and Philology
Comparative Literature
English Language and Literature
   American Literature
   Cultural Studies
   English Literature to 1800
   English Literature since 1800 (including Anglophone)
   Ethnic and Minority American Literature
   Feminist, Gender and Sexuality Studies
   Theory
French and Francophone Language and Literature
   French Linguistics
   French and Francophone Literature
German Language and Literature
   German Linguistics
   German Literature
Global Cultural Studies
   African Studies
   East Asian Studies

Latin American Studies
Near Eastern Studies
Slavic Studies
History
   African
   Asian
   European
   Intellectual History (including History of Culture,
      Science, Technology and Medicine)
   Latin American
   Middle Eastern
   United States
History of Art, Architecture and Archaeology
   American Art
   Ancient, Medieval, Renaissance and Baroque Art and
      Architecture
   Asian Art
   Modern Art
   Theory and Criticism
Music (except performance)
   Ethnomusicology
   Composition
   Musicology
Philosophy
   Epistemology
   Ethics and Political Philosophy
   History of Philosophy
   Metaphysics
   Philosophy of Science
   Epistemology
   Philosophy of Mind and Language
   Philosophy of Science
Religion
Spanish and Portuguese Language and Literature
   Latin American Literature
   Portuguese Literature
   Spanish Linguistics
   Spanish Literature
Theatre and Performance Studies
   History of Theatre and Drama
   Performance Studies
   Theory
Emerging Fields:
   Feminist, Gender, and Sexuality Studies
   Film Studies
   Race, Ethnicity, and Post-Colonial Studies

Appendix F

Fields for Ph.D.s Granted During 1996-2001

Number of Ph.D.s Awarded by
U.S. Institutions, 1996 - 2001

	1996	1997	1998	1999	2000	2001
Life Sciences						
Biochemistry, Biophysics, and Structural Biology*	936	979	966	933	940	888
Cell Biology	280	301	335	314	376	341
Developmental biology	96	115	127	108	111	106
Ecology and Evolutionary Biology*	245	255	293	273	296	336
Genetics, Genomics* and Bioinformatics*	212	217	197	216	227	197
Immunology and Infectious Disease*	260	231	260	236	258	288
Microbiology	460	423	396	396	397	414
Molecular Biology	651	775	736	716	705	707
Neuroscience and Neurobiology*	404	437	413	431	495	482
Pharmacology, Toxicology and Environmental Health	512	547	464	437	442	448
Physiology	275	227	258	244	241	214
Animal Sciences	387	356	341	366	390	332
Entomology	136	123	138	114	137	89
Food Science	149	186	166	144	152	141
Nutrition	142	124	139	102	150	135
Plant Sciences	741	622	729	636	598	545

Physical Sciences, Mathematics and Engineering

	1996	1997	1998	1999	2000	2001
Applied Mathematics	230	242	265	252	238	214
Astrophysics and Astronomy	192	198	207	159	185	186
Chemistry	2148	2148	2216	2132	1989	1979
Computer and Information Sciences	938	923	945	869	876	837
Earth Sciences	421	446	469	420	343	349
Mathematics	696	686	690	643	599	583
Oceanography and Atmospheric Sciences and Meteorology	333	345	316	317	331	279
Physics	1485	1401	1378	1271	1205	1193
Statistics and Probability	259	265	279	250	287	288
Aerospace Engineering	287	273	242	207	215	203
Biological and Agricultural Engineering	104	79	74	59	60	52

Biomedical Engineering	220	211	208	245	251	232
Chemical Engineering	681	662	669	576	619	631
Civil and Environmental Engineering	698	656	650	584	555	593
Electrical and Computer Engineering	1741	1721	1596	1478	1542	1577
Materials Science and Engineering	472	483	482	393	404	450
Mechanical Engineering	1052	1023	1023	855	863	953
Operations Research, Systems Engineering and Industrial Engineering	380	369	359	321	261	306

Social and Behavioral Sciences

Anthropology	418	469	459	489	482	448
Communications	544	470	542	529	533	515
Economics	1179	1164	1158	1077	1090	1087
Geography and Regional Studies	165	149	154	144	197	186
Linguistics	230	244	220	251	229	229
Political Science	721	753	758	774	746	748
Psychology	3497	3562	3676	3673	3618	3433
Sociology	577	626	604	595	680	627

Humanities

American Studies	115	84	100	98	113	127
Classics	72	53	85	77	64	54
Comparative Literature	164	181	164	166	188	203
English Language and Literature	1013	1094	1078	1022	1070	977
French and Francophone Language and Literature	142	150	137	148	143	141
German Language and Literature	88	82	106	90	83	84
Global Cultural Studies	105	101	105	95	108	84
History	857	966	989	1010	1060	1024
History of Art, Architecture and Archaeology	177	188	221	188	228	223
Music (except Performance)	697	727	696	766	748	784
Philosophy	369	446	410	389	364	413
Religion	317	303	327	334	348	343
Spanish and Portuguese* Language and Literature	196	250	207	201	218	233
Theatre and Performance Studies	103	116	92	99	82	104

*Not in National Science Foundation Taxonomy

Source: National Science Foundation, 2001. Unpublished.

Appendix G

Technical and Statistical Techniques

Alternate Ways to Present Rankings:
Random Halves and Bootstrap Methods

Reputational surveys, such as those conducted for earlier research-doctorate program assessments, were not designed to provide accurate rankings of the programs. They represented estimates of ratings, where the results could vary, depending on the selected set of raters. The confidence interval analysis performed in the last two assessments illustrated this point. However, users of the assessments chose to ignore this and focused instead on specific scores obtained by averaging questionnaire responses.

A far better method would be to incorporate variability into the reporting of ratings and display a range of program ratings rather than a single ranking. Random Halves and Bootstrap are two methods which could be used to assign measures of accuracy to statistical estimates as well as to present data. Both methods involve the resampling of original data set in slightly different ways and would provide slightly different results.

Methods

For a particular field, such as English Language and Literature, assume there are M programs and N program raters. Each rater only rates a subset of M programs; therefore, some programs may be rated more often than others, since the number of rating for a program depends on which raters responded to the survey and whether they actually rated a program on their questionnaire. A response matrix **R** can be constructed with a reputational rating r_{ij} as an entry for rater i rating program j, $i = 1,\ldots,N$ and $j = 1,\ldots,M$. Along each of the rows in the matrix there will be blank spaces for programs that the rater was not asked to rate or did not rate. The different ratings for a given program are then aggregated into a single "mean" rating, $\bar{r}_j$ ($\bar{r}_j$ could also include weighting and

trimming, for example, and may not be just the simple mean of all ratings for program j).

Random Halves Method: The Random Halves method is closely related to what is known in statistics literature as the "random group method" for assessing variances of estimates in complex sample surveys. This approach, which has many variants, has literature that goes back to at least 1939 (see Wolter, 1985). It is closely related to another method called the "Jackknife" which was introduced in 1949 and popularized in the 1960s. The essence of the random group or the Jackknife method is to calculate a numerical quantity of interest on a smaller part of the whole data set, and to do this for several such smaller parts of the original data. The differences between the results from these smaller parts of the data are combined to assess the amount of variability, computed on the whole data set. The random halves method is an example of this in which the smaller parts of the whole data are random halves of the data.

The Random Halves method is applied as follows: A random sample of N/2 of the rows of **R** is made without replacement, meaning that a row cannot be selected twice. The mean $\bar{r}_j$ for each program is then computed from this random half sample of the full

data. All the programs are then ranked on a basis of these mean ratings. This procedure could be repeated ten, one hundred, or several hundred times to produce a range of ratings and rankings for each program in the field. Rankings for each program could be summarized as the distribution that lies within the interquartile range of the ratings. Users of reputational ratings would recognize that raters rate programs differently and half of the raters ranked program j from a to b, where a is the 25 percentile of its ranking distribution and b is the 75 percentile.

Bootstrap Method: The Bootstrap method was developed more recently than the random group method, and its literature only dates back to 1979. It is well described in Efron (1982) and Efron and Tibshirani (1993). Although the Bootstrap method was not created specifically for assessing variances in complex sample surveys, it has been used for that purpose. It was created as a general method for assessing the variability of the results of any type of data analysis, complex or simple, and has become a standard tool. Instead of sampling N/2 rows of **R** *without* replacement, N of the rows would be sampled from **R** *with* replacement, meaning that a row could be selected several times. The same procedure could be used for computing the mean, as in the Random Halves method.

The two methods provide very similar results. The perceived advantage in the Random Halves method is in the process, where a rater pool is selected and half the raters are sent questionnaires. This rating process is repeated again and again for the original pool. It is not significantly different from what was done in the past, when the selection of raters and the use of a confidence interval show that a certain percentage of the ratings would fall in a similar interval even if a different set of raters were selected. The advantage in the Bootstrap method, on the other hand, is an established method with a developed theory for the statistical accuracy of survey measurements.

A Comparison of the Random Halves and Bootstrap Methods

The differences between the methods can be demonstrated by the following simple example. Consider an example where three raters rate two programs. The raters are labeled 1, 2 and 3, and the two programs are labeled A and B. The Rating Matrix is:

Table 1: The Rating Matrix

Raters	A	B	Average rating by raters
1	0	1	0.5
2	2	1	1.5
3	1	0	0.5
Average rating	1	2/3	

In this example, all three raters rate the same two programs on a scale of 0 to 2. In turning ratings into rankings, assume that lower ratings correspond to assessments of higher quality. Thus, rater 1 rated A higher than B, by giving A a rating of 0 and B a rating of 1. The last row of the Rating Matrix has the average ratings for each program. For these ratings, B is ranked higher than A because its average rating is slightly lower than that of A. In the discussion of the example, the rank of A, will be denoted by Rank(A). Therefore, Rank(A) = 2, while Rank(B) = 1.

This example may appear to be unrealistic in at least two ways. First, it is very small. This means that it is only possible to examine the probability that A is ranked 1st or 2nd. Second, programs are not sampled for raters to rate, instead, the raters rate *all* of the programs in the example. However, neither of these simplifications is very important for the things that will be demonstrated by the example. On the other hand, the example shows some differences among ratings of the three raters. Rater 1 ranks A and B differently from the way Raters 2 and 3 do. Also the second raters rating numbers are higher than the other two.

In applying Random Halves (RH) to this example, there are two variations, since the number of responses is not an even number. Hence, denote by RH(1) the "half-sample" consists of 1 of the 3 raters chosen at random, and in RH(2) the "half-sample" consists of 2 of the 3 raters chosen at random. These are the only possibilities for the RH method in the example.

In the RH(1) case, since there are three possible raters to be sampled, they are each sampled with probability 1/3, and that the averages are the rating. Below is a table that summarizes the three possible sample results for RH(1).

Table 2: Summary of RH(1)

Sample	Average A rating	Average B rating	Rank(A)	Probability of the sample
{1}	0	1	1	1/3
{2}	2	1	2	1/3
{3}	1	0	2	1/3

Because Rank(A) = 2 in two of the three possible half samples, the probability that Rank(A) = 2 is 2/3. This should be compared to the finding that in the data (i.e., the Rating Matrix on Table 1) the Rank of A is 2, so the RH(1) method indicates that it could have been different from 2 about 1/3 of the time.

In the RH(2) case, two raters are sampled, and there are three possibilities {1,2}, {1,3} and {2,3}. Suppose the two sampled raters are 1 and 2. Then the data to be averaged are given in the following table. The table below summarizes what occurs for three possible half samples for RH(2). Note that in the cases, where the average ratings are the same, random tie splitting is used and the rank order is denoted by 1.5.

Table 3: Summary of RH(2)

Sample	Average A rating	Average B rating	Rank(A)	Probability
{1,2}	1	1	1.5	1/3
{1,3}	1/2	1/2	1.5	1/3
{2,3}	3/2	1/2	2	1/3

In the case of RH(2), there are three ways to get the probability that Rank(A) = 2. The first is from sample {2,3}. The other two ways are either one of two other samples and have the tie split so that Rank (A) = 2. Hence, the probability is 1/3 + (1/3)(1/2) + (1/3)(1/2) = 2/3. The fraction, 1/2, represents the tie splitting. Note that 2/3 is also the probability for Rank(A) = 2 in RH(1).

In summary, the RH method calls for repeatedly taking "half-samples" of the rating matrix, averaging the resulting ratings for A and B, and then ranking A and B based on these average ratings. In resampling over and over, a distribution is constructed of how many times A is ranked 1 or 2. For example, in the case of RH(1) or RH(2), A would be ranked 2 about 2/3^{rds} of the time. Therefore, while the two versions of the RH method give different data, using random tie splitting gives the same results for the probability that A is ranked 2.

Applying the Bootstrap (Boot) method to the example, three raters were sampled, and the same rater could be selected more than once. They were regarded as representative of all the possible raters who could have been sampled to rate the programs. Clearly such an assumption varies in plausibility due to various factors, such as how many raters are being considered and how they are originally chosen. It is, however, a useful assumption and appears throughout many applications of statistics.

In sampling three rows from the original Rating Matrix there are 27 possible combinations or the probability of any sample is 1/27. They are listed in the following table.

Table 4: Bootstrap samples, their average ratings for A and B and the Rank of A.

Sample	A	B	Rank(A)	Sample	A	B	Rank(A)	Sample	A	B	Rank(A)
111	0/3	3/3	1	211	2/3	3/3	1	311	1/3	2/3	1
112	2/3	3/3	1	212	4/3	3/3	2	312	3/3	2/3	2
113	1/3	2/3	1	213	3/3	2/3	2	313	2/3	1/3	2
121	2/3	3/3	1	221	4/3	3/3	2	321	3/3	2/3	2
122	4/3	3/3	2	222	6/3	3/3	2	322	5/3	2/3	2
123	3/3	2/3	2	223	5/3	2/3	2	323	4/3	1/3	2
131	1/3	2/3	1	231	3/3	2/3	2	331	2/3	1/3	2
132	3/3	2/3	2	232	5/3	2/3	2	332	4/3	1/3	2
133	2/3	1/3	2	233	4/3	1/3	2	333	3/3	0/3	2

Rank(A) = 2 occurs a total of 20 times in the table above, yielding a probability of 20/27 = .74. This is different from the results of the RH methods (i.e., .67). However, it is still plausible because while A was ranked second in a sample of 3, there is still some probability that it could have been ranked 1 in a different sample of raters. The Boot method produced a somewhat smaller probability estimate, i.e., .26 rather than .33, so that A could have been ranked 1st, but both of these values are less than ½ and, are both plausible in such a small example.

There is no very convincing, intuitive way to favor either one of these two probability estimates, .67 or .74. Hence, this example has little to offer in making an intuitive choice between the two approaches. What this does show is that the RH and Boot methods do not give the same results for something that is closely related to the types of probabilities. Thus, any claim that the two methods are "equivalent" is wrong, but they are clearly "similar."

Statisticians who are specialists in variance estimation prefer the Bootstrap to ad hoc methods because it is grounded in theory. The Bootstrap method is the nonparametric, maximum likelihood estimate of the probability that Rank(A) = 2. The Random Halves method does not enjoy this property. However, variance estimation is an important subject in statistics and many methods, in particular the Jackknife, can be tailored to situations where they provide serious competition to the Bootstrap. The next section will illustrate that, when the number of raters and programs are both large, there is little difference between the Random Halves and the Bootstrap methods.

Analysis of the Expected Variance for the Two Methods

A natural question to ask is: What do the Random Halves and Boot methods produce for probability distributions of average ratings for programs? Drawing on some results from probability theory it can be shown that these methods give similar results.

Any method of resampling creates random variables with distributions that depend on the resampling method. In the rating example, let the random variables for the average ratings that result for A and B for each sample be denoted by R_A and R_B, respectively. These are random variables with means and variances that have well-known values. The average ratings of A and B in the rating matrix are given in the last row of The Rating Matrix in Table 1, and they are denoted in general as r_A and r_B. Thus, in the example, $r_A = 1$ and $r_B = 2/3$. In addition to the average ratings, the variance of the ratings in each column is defined as the average of the squares of the ratings in each column minus the square of the mean rating for that column. Thus, for program A, the variance is

$$v_A = (0^2 + 2^2 + 1^2)/3 - 1^2 = 5/3 - 1 = 2/3,$$

and, for program B, it is

$$v_B = (1^2 + 1^2 + 0^2)/3 - (2/3)^2 = 2/3 - 4/9 = 6/9 - 4/9 = 2/9.$$

Table 5 gives the results for N raters rating Program A and n raters used in the RH(n) method. If N is even, then n = N/2. In the table let $E(R_A)$ denote the "expected value" or "long-run average value" of the average rating for A, R_A. Statistics show that it is the same value, r_A, for both the Boot and the RH methods. r_A is also the average rating for A in the original Rating Matrix, and in general, r_A is the average rating given to program A by the raters rating it. Thus, both the RH and Boot methods are unbiased for r_A, and any sensible resampling method will share this property.

Table 5: The mean and variance of the average rating for A in a single resample

	Bootstrap Method	**Random Halves, RH(n), Method**
$E(R_A)$	r_A	r_A
$Var(R_A)$	$\dfrac{v_A}{N}$	$\dfrac{v_A}{n}\dfrac{(N-n)}{(N-1)}$

Where the two methods can differ is in the value of the variance, $Var(R_A)$. This variance is a measure of how much R_A deviates on average from the mean value, r_A, from one random resampling to another. Observe that both formulas for $Var(R_A)$ involve, v_A, the variance of the ratings in the column of the Rating Matrix for program A. Note that when N is even, and $n = N/2$ then the $N - n$ in the numerator for RH(n) is n and it cancels the n in the denominator leaving only $N - 1$ in the denominator. This is to be compared to the N in the denominator for the Bootstrap method. When N, the number of raters is large, then N and N-1 are close and the variances of average rating, R_A, for the two methods are nearly the same.

The factor or the right side of the formula for the RH(n) variance is known as the finite sampling correction and it gets smaller as n increases relative to N. In the simple example, here is what these formulas yield.

RH(1): In this case, R_A takes on these three possible values with the corresponding probabilities.

Possible average ratings	0	1	2
Probabilities	1/3	1/3	1/3

The mean of this distribution is $0(1/3) + 1(1/3) + 2(1/3) = 1 = r_A$.

Its variance is $0^2(1/3) + 1^2(1/3) + 2^2(1/3) - 1^2 = 2/3$.

Applying the formula for the variance for RH(1) from Table 5 gives

$((2/3)/1)(3 - 1)/(3 - 1) = 2/3$, the same value.

RH(2): In this case, R_A takes on these three possible values with the corresponding probabilities.

Possible average ratings	1/2	1	3/2
Probabilities	1/3	1/3	1/3

The mean of this distribution is $(1/2)(1/3) + 1(1/3) + (3/2)(1/3) = 1 = r_A$, as before.

Its variance is $(1/2)^2(1/3) + (1)^2(1/3) + (3/2)^2(1/3) - 1^2$
$= ((1/4) + 1 + (9/4))/3 - 1 = (14/4)/3 - (12/12) = 2/12 = 1/6.$

Applying the formula for the variance for RH(2) from Table 7 gives

$((2/3)/2)(3 - 2)/(3 - 1) = (1/3)(1/2) = 1/6$, the same value.

Boot: In this case, R_A takes on seven possible values with the corresponding probabilities.

Possible average ratings	0	1/3	2/3	1	4/3	5/3	2
Probabilities	1/27	3/27	6/27	7/27	6/27	3/37	1/3

These probabilities are found by summing up the Bootstrap samples that yield the given possible value in Table 4. This is a larger set of possible average ratings for A than either one of the RH methods gives. This is due to the richer set of samples available under the Boot method.

The mean of this distribution is $(0)(1/27) + (1/3)(3/27) + (2/3)(6/27) + (1)(7/27) +$
$(4/3)(6/27) + (5/3)(3/27) + (2)(1/27) = 1 = r_A$, as it is for the other two methods.

The variance is $(0)^2(1/27) + (1/3)^2(3/27) + (2/3)^2(6/27) + (1)^2(7/27) + (4/3)^2(6/27) +$
$(5/3)^2(3/27) + (2)^2(1/27) - 1^2 = (1/9)(1/27)(3 + 24 + 63 + 96 + 75 + 36) - 1 =$
$(297/(9x27)) - 1 = (11/9) - (9/9) = 2/9.$

Applying the formula for the variance for Boot from Table 5 gives

$((2/3)/3) = 2/9$, the same value.

Summary of results

The mean and variance calculations as applied to this simple example illustrates the following:

   (a) The RH and Boot methods are only similar when N, the number of raters rating a program, is large enough to make the difference between N and N – 1 negligible.
   (b) The set of possible samples from which resampling takes place differs for the two methods, the one for method Boot is much larger in general.
   (c) Both methods are unbiased for the mean rating of a program, but they differ in their variances. When N is even, the variance of Boot is smaller, when N is odd, the variance of Boot lies between that for RH(n) and RH(n+1) where n < N/2 < n+1. This is observed by examining the data in Table 4.
   (d) The Boot method usually has a much richer set of possible ratings in its resampling distribution, and fewer ties.

References.

Wolter, K. M. 1985. *Introduction to Variance Estimation*. New York: Springer-Verlag.

Efron, B. 1982. *The Jackknife, the Bootstrap and other Resampling Plans*. Philadelphia: Society for Industrial and Applied Mathematics.

Efron, B., and Tibshirani, R. J. 1993. *An Introduction to the Bootstrap*. New York: Chapman & Hall.

Correlates of Reputation Analysis

The reputational quality of a program is a purely subjective measure; however, it is related to quantitative measures in the sense that quality judgment could be made on the basis of information about programs, such as the scholarly work of the faculty and the honors awarded to the faculty for that scholarship. Therefore, it may be possible to relate or to predict quality rankings for programs using quantitative measures. It is clear that predicted quality rankings would also be subjective and that the accuracy of such predictions may change over time.

One way to construct such a relationship is to do a least squares multilinear regression. The dependent variable in the regression analysis is represented by a set of average ratings, $r_1, r_2, . . , r_N$ for N programs in a particular field. The predictors or independent variables would be a set of quantitative or coded program characteristics that are represented by a vector, x_n, for program n. The analysis would construct a function $f(x)$ which provides a *predicted* average rating $f(x_n)$ for program n. In this case the relation between r_n and $f(x_n)$ would be

$$r_n = f(x_n) + e_n = a_1x_{1,n} + a_2x_{2,n} + . . . + a_mx_{m,n} + a_{m+1} + e_n \qquad (1)$$

where $x_{1,n}, x_{2,n}, ..., x_{m,n}$ represent the m quantity or coded characteristics for the program n in the field, and e_n, is the residual or the amount by which the predicted average rating varies from the actual average rating for that program. If the prediction is "good" then the residuals are relatively small. The coefficients a_j are determined by minimizing the sum of the squares of the differences $r_n - f(x_n)$.

While a single regression equation is generated using quantitative data and the reputational score, the selected raters of the program provide a certain amount of variability. This variability can be shown in the following manner: Associated with each coefficient a_i is a 95%-confidence interval $[L_i, U_i]$, and by randomly selecting values for the coefficients within their confidence intervals, a predicted average rating $\acute{r}_n$ can be generated for program n. A measure of how close the set of $\acute{r}_n$ ratings is to the r_n ratings can be calculated by

$$\| \acute{r} - r \|^2 < p\, s^2\, F, \qquad (2)$$

where $\acute{r} = (\acute{r}_1, \acute{r}_2, ... , \acute{r}_N)$, $r = (r_1, r_2, ..., r_N)$ and $\| \ \|^2$ denotes the sum of squares of the components of the difference vector. The bound on the inequality, $p\, s^2\, F$, is a constant that is derived from the regression analysis.

p = m, the number of nonconstant terms in the regression equation,
s^2 is the "mean square for error" given in the output of a regression program, and
F = the 95% cutoff point for the F-distribution with p and n-p degrees of freedom.

By repeating the random selection of coefficients many times, a collection of coefficients can be determined that satisfies inequality (2), and the upper- and lower-bounds of this collection defines an interval [L'$_i$, U'$_i$]. For coefficients in these intervals a range of predicted ratings can be generated.

From the practical point of a program trying to estimate the quality of its program, a few years after a reputational survey is conducted, it could use a linear regression equation with coefficients in [L'$_i$, U'$_i$] to generate a new range of ratings based on current program data, or if data for all programs in the field were available, a new interquartile ranking of programs could be obtained.

The following is an example where this method is applied to the 1995 ratings of programs in Mathematics.

Mathematics

Using the STATA statistical package and applying a forward stepwise, least-squares linear regression on a large number of quantitative variables which characterized publications, citations, faculty size and rank, research grant support, number of doctorates by gender and race/ethnicity, graduate students by gender, graduate student support, and time to degree, the following seven variables were identified as being the most significant:

(ginipub)   Gini Coefficient for Program Publications, 1988-92: The Gini coefficient is an indicator of the concentration of publications on a small number of the program faculty during the period 1988-92.

(phds)   Total Number of Doctorates FY 86-92

(perfull)   Percentage of Full Professors Participating in the Program

(persupp)   Percentage of Program Faculty with Research Support (1986-92)

(perfpub)   Percentage of Program Faculty Publishing in the Period 1988-1992

(ratiocit)   Ratio of the Total Number of Program Citations in the Period 1988-1992 to the Number of Program Faculty

(myd)   Median Time Lapse from Entering Graduate School to Receipt of Ph.D. in Years

Results of a regression analysis are shown below. About 95% of the variation is explained by these variables, where $R^2 = 0.8304$.

```
    Source |       SS       df       MS              Number of obs =     139
-----------+------------------------------           F(  7,   131) =   91.60
     Model | 112.36003       7  16.0514329           Prob > F      =  0.0000
  Residual |  22.954789     131  .175227397          R-squared     =  0.8304
-----------+------------------------------           Adj R-squared =  0.8213
     Total | 135.314819     138  .98054217           Root MSE      =   .4186
```

```
----------------------------------------------------------------------
   quality |      Coef.   Std. Err.       t    P>|t|     [95% Conf. Interval]
-----------+----------------------------------------------------------
      phds |    .3489197   .0544665     6.41   0.000      .2411721    .4566674
   perfull |     .008572   .0027864     3.08   0.003      .0030598    .0140842
   persupp |    .0183162   .0025146     7.28   0.000      .0133418    .0232906
   perfpub |   -.0150464   .0035235    -4.27   0.000     -.0220167   -.0080762
   ratiocit |    .0258671   .0077198     3.35   0.001      .0105955    .0411387
       myd |   -.7737551   .1995707    -3.88   0.000    -1.168553   -.3789567
   ginipub |   -.0294944   .0044222    -6.67   0.000     -.0382425   -.0207462
     _cons |    3.070145   .3625634     8.47   0.000      2.352908    3.787382
----------------------------------------------------------------------
```

The resulting predictor equation is:

$$f(x) = 3.07 + 0.349(phds) + 0.009(perfull) + 0.018(persupp) - 0.015(perfpub) + 0.026(ratiocit) - .774(myd) - 0.029(ginipub)$$

It is noted that the Root Mean Square Error (RMSE) from the regression is 0.4186, and the variation in scores from the 1995 confidence interval calculation has an RMSE of 0.2277.

The following is scatter plot of the actual 1995 ratings and the predicted ratings.

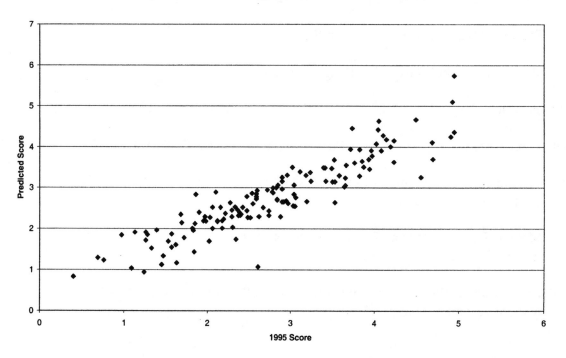

Plot of the Predicted Faculty Quality Score Against the Actual 1995 Score for Programs in Mathematics

The 95%-confidence interval for each of the variables used in the regression can now be used to find a new estimate for the quality score. As described above, values for the coefficients in the regression equation are randomly selected in the intervals and tested to see if that set of coefficients satisfies the relation $\| \dot{r} - r \|^2 < p\, s^2\, F$. For Mathematics data the bound $p\, s^2\, F = (7)(.4186)^2(2.12) = 2.563556$. For this example 3,000 random selections were made in the coefficient intervals and 220 coefficients sets satisfied the inequality. The corresponding maximum and minimum interval are:

	phds coefficient	persupp coefficient	ginipub coefficient	myd coefficient	perfpub coefficient	ratiocit coefficient	perfull coefficient	constant
Max	0.35469	0.018583	-0.029026	-0.7526	-0.014673	0.026686	0.0088674	3.10858
Min	0.34314	0.018049	-0.029964	-0.79495	-0.015421	0.025047	0.0082761	3.03164

Using the values in the above table, the maximum and minimum predicted quality scores can be calculated, and the scores for Mathematics programs are displayed in the table below.

As described earlier, these maximum and minimum coefficient values could be used to construct new quality scores, by randomly selecting the coefficients in the regression equation between the corresponding maximum and minimum values. If this is done repeatedly a collection of quality scores is obtained for each program and the interquartile range of this collection could be generated. This was done 100 times and the results are given as the Predicted Ranks in the table with the Bootstrap rankings.

Institution	Quality Score Maximum	Quality Score Minimum	Predicted Ranks 1st Quartile	Predicted Ranks 3rd Quartile	Bootstrap Ranks 1st Quartile	Bootstrap Ranks 3rd Quartile
Dartmouth College	2.73	2.51	73	76	53	62
Boston University	2.70	2.42	77	80	48	52
Brandeis University	3.17	2.88	49	51	32	36
Harvard University	4.41	4.09	8	9	2	4
Massachusetts Inst of Technology	5.27	4.93	2	2	3	4
U of Massachusetts at Amherst	3.40	3.11	38	40	54	60
Northeastern University	2.41	2.13	99	103	70	80
Brown University	4.60	4.31	5	6	26	29
Brown University-Applied Math	4.59	4.26	6	6	14	17
University of Rhode Island	1.69	1.40	128	129	122	125
University of Connecticut	2.66	2.39	79	83	98	102
Wesleyan University	2.31	2.09	104	107	101	110
Yale University	3.38	3.13	38	40	7	8
Adelphi University	1.07	0.82	138	138	130	133
CUNY - Grad Sch & Univ Center	3.38	3.10	40	41	30	32
Clarkson University	2.49	2.21	90	94	109	118
Columbia University	4.32	3.99	11	11	10	12
Cornell University	4.81	4.46	3	4	14	16
New York University	4.83	4.50	3	4	7	8
Polytechnic University	2.15	1.88	112	114	98	105
Rensselaer Polytechnic Inst	3.64	3.36	27	30	48	52
University of Rochester	3.10	2.83	52	54	56	62

State Univ of New York-Albany	2.55	2.33	85	88	82	90
State Univ of New York-Binghamton	2.55	2.33	85	87	65	75
State Univ of New York-Buffalo	3.00	2.76	57	59	61	70
State Univ of New York-Stony Brook	3.60	3.31	30	32	19	22
Syracuse University	2.42	2.18	95	100	76	84
Princeton University	4.52	4.21	7	7	2	3
Rutgers State Univ-New Brunswick	4.06	3.77	16	18	17	20
Stevens Inst of Technology	1.73	1.48	127	127	121	128
Carnegie Mellon University	3.63	3.33	28	31	34	40

English Language and Literature

Applying the same method to the 1995 programs in English Language and Literature, a slightly different result is obtained, since programs in this field do not have the same productivity characteristics as those in Mathematics. Again, forward stepwise least squares linear regression was applied to a large number of quantitative variables, and the following were identified as being the most significant:

(nopubs2)   Number of Publications During the Period 1985-1992

(perfawd)   Percentage of Program Faculty with at Least One Honor or Award for the Period 1986-1992

(acadplan)   Total Number of Doctorates FY 1986-1992 with academic employment plans at the 4-year college or university level.

(ginicit)   Gini Coefficienticient for Program Citations, 1988-1992: The Gini coefficienticient is an indicator of the concentration of citations on a small number of the program faculty during the period 1988-1992.

(nocits1)   Number of Citations During the Period 1981-1992

(fullprof)   Percentage of Full Professors Participating in the Program

(empplan)   Total Number of Doctorates FY 1986-1992 with Employment Plans.

None of the variables identified in the Mathematics regression are present in this regression analysis.

Results of this regression analysis are shown below. About 95% of the variation is explained by these variables, where $R^2 = 0.8106$.

Source	SS	df	MS
Model	83.985691	7	11.9979559
Residual	19.6227839	109	.18002554
Total	103.608475	116	.893176507

Number of obs = 117
F(7, 109) = 66.65
Prob > F = 0.0000
R-squared = 0.8106
Adj R-squared = 0.7984
Root MSE = .42429

q93a	Coef.	Std. Err.	t	P>|t|	[95% Conf. Interval]	
nopubs2	.1202936	.1017753	1.18	0.240	-.0814218	.322009
perfawd	.0326877	.0041423	7.89	0.000	.0244777	.0408977
acadplan	.7961931	.2416467	3.29	0.001	.3172573	1.275129
ginicit	-.0007486	.0001839	-4.07	0.000	-.001113	-.0003842
nocits1	.0827859	.0234272	3.53	0.001	.036354	.1292178
fullprof	.2942413	.1096454	2.68	0.008	.0769276	.511555
empplan	-.599897	.2698761	-2.22	0.028	-1.134783	-.0650113
_cons	1.955276	.1533968	12.75	0.000	1.651249	2.259304

The resulting predictor equation is:

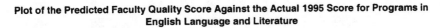

$$f(x) = 1.955 + 0.12(\text{nopubs2}) + 0.033(\text{perfawd}) + 0.796(\text{acadplan})$$
$$-0.001(\text{ginicit}) + 0.083(\text{nocits1}) + 0.294(\text{fullprof}) - 0.6(\text{empplan}).$$

The following is a scatter plot of the Random Halves draw from the 1995 rankings and the predicted ranking for that draw.

For programs in English Language and Literature, the Root Mean Square Error (RMSE) from the regression is 0.42429, and the variation in scores from the 1995 confidence interval calculation has an RMSE of 0.2544.

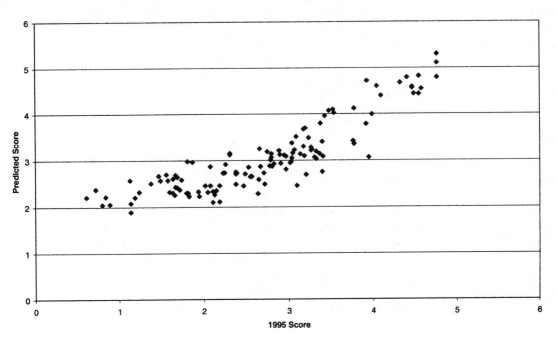

Plot of the Predicted Faculty Quality Score Against the Actual 1995 Score for Programs in English Language and Literature

In Mathematics the 95%-confidence interval for each of the variables used in the regression can be used to determine a new estimate for the quality score. In this case, the bound $p \ s^2 \ F = (7)(.42869)^2(2.18) = 2.747136$. For this example 3,000 random selections were also made in the coefficient intervals and 242 coefficients sets satisfied the inequality. The corresponding maximum and minimum intervals are:

	nopubs2 coefficient	perfawd coefficient	acadplan coefficient	ginicit coefficient	nocits coefficient	fullprof coefficient	empplan coefficient	constant
Max	0.13384	0.033239	0.82835	-0.00072	0.085903	0.30883	-0.56399	1.97569
Min	0.10684	0.03214	0.76425	-0.00077	0.079689	0.27975	-0.63557	1.935

For the example used with Mathematics programs, the maximum and minimum values for the coefficients can be used to calculate the maximum and minimum predicted quality scores for the programs in English Language and Literature. These scores are displayed in the table below.

Repeating the exercise, described for Mathematics, of randomly selecting coefficient values in the maximum-minimum intervals a large number of times, an interquartile range can be generated for programs in English Language and Literature. This was again done 100 times and the results are given as the Predicted Ranks in the table with the Random Halves rankings.

Institution	Quality Score		Predicted Ranking		Random Halves Ranks	
	Maximum	Maximum	1st Quartile	3rd Quartile	1st Quartile	3rd Quartile
University of New Hampshire	2.74	2.56	91	93	70	77
Boston College	2.57	2.42	96	98	59	64
Boston University	3.80	3.59	20	21	38	42
Brandeis University	3.63	3.40	19	21	44	55
Harvard University	5.55	5.05	1	1	2	3
U of Massachusetts at Amherst	3.84	3.51	30	34	38	43
Tufts University	2.35	2.22	108	110	67	74
Brown University	4.21	3.78	15	16	13	15
University of Rhode Island	2.39	2.22	113	115	94	113
University of Connecticut	3.26	3.05	53	57	79	87
Yale University	5.07	4.52	5	6	2	3
CUNY - Grad Sch & Univ Center	3.50	3.21	42	48	18	19
Columbia University	4.90	4.24	9	10	7	9
Cornell University	4.71	4.16	13	13	6	8
St John's University	1.93	1.86	127	127	119	122
Fordham University	2.38	2.23	103	106	104	112
New York University	3.59	3.25	26	28	18	20
Drew University	2.30	2.15	116	119	123	126
University of Rochester	3.30	3.02	30	33	44	48
State Univ of New York-Binghamton	3.01	2.72	62	64	65	69

State Univ of New York-Buffalo	3.65	3.16	30	37	25	27
State U of New York-Stony Brook	3.17	2.77	48	55	46	52
Syracuse University	2.53	2.38	95	98	71	76
Indiana Univ of Pennsylvania	2.19	1.93	124	126	122	124
Princeton University	4.82	4.39	5	6	12	14
Rutgers State Univ-New Brunswick	3.96	3.62	22	23	16	18
Carnegie Mellon University	3.17	3.01	33	35	52	54